Standardized Testing Issues

Teachers' Perspectives

Standardized
Testing
Issues

Teachers' Perspectives

Reference & Resource Series

National Education Association
Washington, D.C.

Stock No. 1501-0-00

Note

The opinions expressed in this publication should not be construed as representing the policy or position of the National Education Association. Materials published as part of the *NEA Reference & Resource Series* are intended to be discussion documents for teachers who are concerned with specialized interests of the profession.

Library of Congress Cataloging in Publication Data

National Education Association of the United
    States.
    Standardized testing issues.

    (Reference and resource series)
    Includes bibliographical references.
    1. Examinations—United States.   I. Title.
II. Series.
LB3051.N3 1977   372.1'2'6   77-24041
ISBN 0-8106-1501-0

Acknowledgments

"Glossary of Measurement Terms" (in "Guidelines and Cautions for Considering Criterion-Referenced Testing" by Bernard McKenna) is excerpted from the revised edition of *A Glossary of Measurement Terms: A Basic Vocabulary for Evaluation and Testing*, published by CTB/McGraw-Hill, Del Monte Research Park, Monterey, California 93940. Reprinted by permission of the publisher.

The following articles are reprinted with permission from *Today's Education:*

    "An Alternative to Blanket Standardized Testing" by Richard J. Stiggins.

    "Criticisms of Standardized Testing" by Milton G. Holmen and Richard F. Docter.

    "The Looking-Glass World of Testing" by Edwin F. Taylor.

    "One Way It Can Be" by Brenda S. Engel.

    "A Summary of Alternatives"

    "A Teacher Views Criterion-Referenced Tests" by Jean S. Blachford.

    "Teacher-Made Tests—An Alternative to Standardized Tests" by Frances Quinto.

    "The Testing of Minority Children—A Neo-Piagetian Approach" by Edward A. De Avila and Barbara Havassy.

    "The Way It Is" by Charlotte Darehshori.

    "What's Wrong with Standardized Testing?" by Bernard McKenna.

CONTENTS

"Girl number twenty," said Mr. Gradgrind, squarely pointing with his square forefinger, "I don't know that girl. Who is that girl?"

"Sissy Jupe, sir," explained number twenty, blushing, standing up, and curtseying.

"Sissy is not a name," said Mr. Gradgrind. "Don't call yourself Sissy. Call yourself Cecilia."

"It's father as calls me Sissy, sir," returned the young girl in a trembling voice, and with another curtsey.

"Then he has no business to do it," said Mr. Gradgrind. "Tell him he mustn't. Cecilia Jupe. Let me see. What is your father?"

"He belongs to the horse-riding [the circus], if you please, sir."

Mr. Gradgrind frowned, and waved off the objectionable calling with his hand.

"We don't want to know anything about that, here. You mustn't tell us about that, here. Your father breaks horses, don't he?"

"If you please, sir, when they can get any to break, they do break horses in the ring, sir."

"You mustn't tell us about the ring here. Very well, then. Describe your father as a horsebreaker. He doctors sick horses, I dare say?"

"Oh, yes, sir."

"Very well, then. He is a veterinary surgeon, a farrier, and horsebreaker. Give me your definition of a horse."

(Sissy Jupe thrown into the greatest alarm by this demand.)

"Girl number twenty unable to define a horse!" said Mr. Gradgrind, for the general behoof of all the little pitchers. "Girl number twenty possessed of no facts in reference to one of the commonest of animals! Some boy's definition of a horse." . . . .

* * * * * *

"Bitzer," said Thomas Gradgrind. "Your definition of a horse."

"Quadruped. Graminivorous. Forty teeth, namely twenty-four grinders, four eye-teeth, and twelve incisive. Sheds coat in the spring; in marshy countries, sheds hoofs, too. Hoofs hard, but requiring to be shod with iron. Age known by marks in mouth." Thus (and much more) Bitzer.

"Now, girl number twenty," said Mr. Gradgrind, "you know what a horse is."

—from Book the First, "Sowing": Chapter Two, "Murdering the Innocents" of Hard Times by Charles Dickens (1854).

WHAT'S WRONG WITH STANDARDIZED TESTING?
by Bernard McKenna

In the social sciences, economics is known as the dismal science. In education the "dismal science" has to be standardized testing.

- Its history is ominous.
- Much test content is unimportant or irrelevant.
- The structure and formats of the tests are confusing and misleading.
- The process of administering the tests is demeaning, wasteful of time, and counterproductive.
- The application of statistics that result from test scores distorts reality.
- It is difficult, if not impossible, to ensure that test results will be used either to improve student learning or to help teachers improve instruction.

The paragraphs that follow develop each of these points.

Intelligence and achievement testing began in the United States about the turn of the century and is closely associated with developments in France. The story is well known of how the French minister of public instruction commissioned Alfred Binet to construct a test to identify students whose aptitudes were so low that they should be placed in special schools. Binet soon found himself opposing those philosophers who supported the idea that intelligence is a fixed quantity. He said, "We must protest and react against this brutal pessimism."[1]

But the Americans who were influential in bringing the Binet test to America, Lewis Terman of Stanford University and Henry Goddard of the Vineland Training School in New Jersey, espoused the "brutal pessimism." Terman's translation became the widely used Stanford-Binet IQ Test.

The U.S. Public Health Service commissioned Goddard to administer the Binet test to immigrants at the receiving station on Ellis Island. The test results "showed" that 87 percent of Russians, 83 percent of Jews, 80 percent of Hungarians, and 79 percent of Italians were feebleminded. Conse-quently, the percentage of aliens deported for feeblemindedness rose by 350 percent in 1913. A history to be proud of? A record leading to enlightenment? For shame!

The next gathering of destructive test data was during World War I when mental tests were given en masse to draftees. Analysis of these results immediately following the war resulted in their dis-criminatory use against Blacks—to demonstrate that Blacks had lower IQs than Whites. And so it goes. Between then and now is a history of further "refinement" of essentially the same content and formats, of the misuse and abuse of the same kinds of IQ tests that so destructively dealt with immi-grants and minority groups in the early 1900's and during World War I.

The history of standardized achievement testing is only slightly less dismal than that of IQ tests. Edward L. Thorndike developed the first formal achievement tests in 1904. The main reason for achievement testing was not to assess student progress or improve teaching but to establish the profession of psychology as a science separate from philosophy. Never mind the students and teachers and their needs. The psychologists saw the oppor-tunity to be considered scientists if they came up with precise measuring tools with which to ply their trade. Thorndike wrote that "the nature of educational measurement is the same as that of all scientific measurement." And so the course was set, a course that has never been reversed: The evaluation of student progress would be considered in the same realm with measuring tolerances of automobile pistons or the trajectory of missiles.

The near panic among the American public created by Russia's launching of the Sputnik in 1957 led to vastly increased testing programs. This overemphasis on the use of tests resulted in several published warnings of the dangers of such pro-liferation. *Testing Testing Testing,* by a joint com-mittee of national educational associations, and *The Tyranny of Testing,* by Banesh Hoffmann, were among them. But these warnings went un-heeded. And before the end of the 60's, evaluation guidelines of Title I of the Elementary and Secondary Education Act resulted in even more standardized testing.

By the early 1970's, the situation had become so oppressive that warnings were once again heralded. A national task force of the National Education Association and two substantive and penetrating issues of the *National Elementary Principal* (March-April 1975, July-August 1975) were among those sounding the alarm. Even as this article goes to press, the *Reader's Digest* carries a warning piece on the potential dangers of standardized testing—and a report out of London discredits a British psychologist's studies of identical twins, a major source for the conclusion that IQ is innate.

At the same time a movement called performance-based education calls for more testing, much of which is or promises to become standardized in one form or another. One is reminded of the refrain, "When will they ever learn, when will they ever learn?"

Ralph Tyler's observation that standardized tests get "small answers to small questions" is apt. The content of the tests evaluates little more than the ability to recall facts, define words, and do routine calculations. Obviously, not all these things are unimportant, but even in the reading and mathematics parts of these tests, many of the questions are inane. The mathematics sections emphasize mechanical calculation at a time when inexpensive electronic calculators are available to the general public. And the tests make almost no provision for evaluating a student's ability to estimate or to measure real things—important skills needed for functioning as workers and citizens. As one prominent mathematician has put it, "The concepts sections of most of the commonly used achievement tests suffer from the fact that they trivialize the concepts." Large percentages of the items in standardized tests, particularly in IQ tests, are limited to word definitions, all of which are learnable and tell little about students' general aptitudes. Further, the words to be defined are often obscure, infrequently used or encountered in reading, writing, and speaking.

If the content of the basic skills tests and IQ tests is poor, that in the social studies is infinitely worse. For example, the social-studies part of one nationally prominent test reflects little of contemporary curriculum change and improvement in this subject area. One review states that it totally neglects "the art of discovery" and "process," both very much a part of accepted teaching strategies today. And of science test items, a scientist-researcher says, "They are incorrect, misleading, skewed in emphasis, and irrelevant."

The content of standardized tests emphasizes getting "right answers," almost totally neglecting the thought process by which the answers are arrived at. Interestingly, a recent Gallup poll indicates that a major educational concern of parents is that the schools help students think for themselves.

Much else that is wrong with the substance of standardized tests can be only briefly cited here:

- Test content does not reflect local instructional objectives or specific curriculums.
- Much of the content is unimportant or irrelevant to anything students need to know or understand.
- Test content measures mainly recall-type learning, neglecting the higher thought processes—analyzing, synthesizing, and drawing generalizations and applying them to new phenomena.
- The tests give an incomplete picture of student learning progress, because items that all or almost all students have learned are removed from the tests in order to keep the norming procedure statistically sound.
- The test maker uses a language that is not commonly used in other activities in the real world.
- Test items are unduly complex and require too many different manipulations; sometimes instructions for the items are unclear.
- Test vocabularies and illustrations are often unfamiliar to those who are not of white middle-class cultures or for whom English is a second language; that is, the tests are culturally and linguistically biased.

The test formats are unimaginative, restrictive of creative thinking, and confusing. The multiple-choice mentality that is sometimes referred to in jest ("A, B, C, or none of the above") is more than a cliché. Large numbers of items in most standardized tests are multiple-choice. The assertion that students become more able to think for themselves by learning to respond to multiple-choice items offers a simplistic solution to a complex problem. In fact, there is some evidence that the reverse is true. Because each multiple-choice item must appear somewhat plausible as an answer in order to minimize guessing, more than one answer can often be logically assumed to be right. This works particular hardships on those who think most creatively and innovatively.

Because of space limitations, test illustrations and pictures frequently are out of proportion: An eraser is about the same size as an automobile, houses are smaller than people, etc.

The need for speed in taking the tests imposes an artificial structure that is not characteristic of real-life tasks. Obviously, students need to learn to work rapidly and accurately. But in the real world, not much is comparable to answering 40 multiple-choice items in 60 minutes, or whatever.

Standardized testing uses up inordinate amounts of precious instructional time. Thousands of hours go into testing that might better be used in individualizing instruction and planning for teaching. In terms of cost efficiency, the testing business runs into hundreds of millions of dollars, the results of which provide little or no help to students and teachers.

Testing situations generate fear, imply mistrust, and generally threaten and demean students. The emphasis on competition, the pressure of time, and the measures used to discourage cheating cause students to have lowered self-concepts and to feel insecure and mistrusted.

Testing settings are frequently physically intolerable: Time periods of testing are too long, instructions are blared out on public address systems, and large groups of students are herded into cafeterias or auditoriums where they work on their laps.

In spite of the evidence, the test makers say that there isn't much wrong with the content, structure, and formats of the tests. And while they admit that there are abuses in reporting, interpreting, and using the results, they assume little responsibility for this. They argue that if administrators and teachers would just interpret and use the results properly everything would be all right. Well, everything wouldn't be all right.

Surely practitioners can improve test interpretation and usage, but proper interpretation and usage are almost unattainable because of the kind of substance and formats mentioned in the preceding paragraphs. It is nearly impossible to separate content and structure from usage—content and structure, in large part, determine usage.

Even if it were possible to separate content and structure from usage, large problems of usage would still remain. Let us examine some of them.

The standardization process in testing leads to reporting of results in terms of averages (norms). This distribution of scores along a range ensures that half the students will be below average no matter how well they do. Since there is nothing beyond subjective judgment to determine how "good" average (or above or below average) is, it is possible that "below average" represents good progress on some tests and "above average" represents poor programs on others.

On the matter of interpretation of results, a major fault with standardized testing is attributing to the findings much more meaning than they deserve—assuming that verbal and quantitative scores stand for general intelligence, for example. Guilford and his associates confirmed long ago that the intellect has many dimensions, of which verbal and quantitative abilities are only a part.

The statement of a prominent psychometrist that if she had just one measure of intelligence it would be vocabulary represents the kind of narrow point of view about interpreting test scores that does disservice to both those who are tested and those who use scores to make decisions that may affect human beings throughout their lives. On the achievement-test side, a student's ability (or inability) to respond "correctly" to more than half the items on a standardized achievement test in biology or social studies tells too little of his or her potential in either of these subjects to be a basis for broad-range decision making.

Yet decisions are made regularly on such narrow data, decisions that may limit or deny students' opportunities. On the basis of standardized tests results, students are categorized, grouped, and pigeonholed; placed in classes for the retarded; excluded from particular courses of study; prohibited from pursuing advanced programs; barred from particular institutions; and even denied job opportunities. And all this, sometimes on as small a basis as two or three wrong answers, answers to questions that themselves may be highly questionable.

Even when test results are not used in formal decision-making processes, they affect practitioners' expectations of particular students. "Mary is in the lower quartile. There is not much use spending time on her; she just doesn't have it," is an attitude that test results create. But Mary may "have it," and the reasons for the low test scores may have been the particular testing situation or Mary's physical or emotional situation at testing time. Or Mary may "have it" in many ways not evaluated by the tests. But since the tests themselves create the impression that they measure what's important or most of what's important, Mary may not get much attention after scoring low on them.

Decision making on the basis of standardized test scores goes far beyond the classroom. School administrators use test scores in comparing classrooms and school buildings and make decisions on programs and personnel accordingly, school boards and legislatures use scores to determine the allocation of resources, and the public judges the overall quality of education on the basis of the scores they read about in the papers. None of these uses is appropriate. All of them assume that the tests indicate much more than any group-administered standardized test is capable of.

Most important, for students and teachers, the test results are too broad and general to provide diagnosis of individual student learning problems, and they don't help teachers select the most appropriate teaching methodologies for individual students or groups of students.

The schools and colleges of America should not use group-administered norm-referenced standardized intelligence, aptitude, and achievement tests. As Jerold Zacharias, prominent physicist and professor emeritus at Massachusetts Institute of Technology, pointed out in the *National Elementary Principal,* it is not sufficient to "retreat to catch phrases like 'I know these tests are not very good, but they are all we have.' There are many other ways to assess a child's general competence. They may not look numerical or scientific, but they are known to every teacher and every school principal who reads this journal."

Among such other ways are objectives-referenced (criterion-referenced) tests of which teacher-made tests are a part, individual diagnostic instruments, interviews of students to determine their progress and learning needs, evaluation of the products of student work and their live performances, simulation, contracts with students, student self-evaluation, and peer evaluation.

Almost no one wants less rigorous evaluation of student-learning progress. If the American schools are to respond effectively to agreed-on goals and objectives, more and better evaluation procedures will be required. *But one thing is certain: Large-scale mass-administered standardized testing programs will not accomplish this mission.*

Most teachers are well aware of this. They need to use their expertise, professional judgment, and influence with other educators and the public to end such testing programs in their school systems. And individually and collectively, they need to influence the testing industry, state education departments, and other groups to reallocate their large resources to research, develop, field test, and disseminate a broad range of alternatives to standardized tests for evaluating student learning progress and to help teachers improve instruction.

THE LOOKING-GLASS WORLD OF TESTING
by Edwin F. Taylor

Take a look at this multiple-choice question:

Scientists study three basic kinds of things—animals, vegetables, and

    people
    stars
    minerals
    foods
    religions

"Animal, vegetable, or mineral" is a way to divide up the world in the game "20 Questions." It has nothing to do with what scientists study. In fact, scientists study (among other things) people *and* stars *and* minerals *and* foods *and* (if you include archaeology) religions. The description of science implied but this test question is nonsense. No sense.

That question is from a standardized achievement test for elementary school children. (We'll mention later the meanings of *standardized* and *achievement.)*

Now look at this question from another test:

If ½ of 6 is 3, then ¼ of 8 is _____ .

Never mind the answer (which is also presented as multiple-choice): What does the question mean? *If . . . then . . .* usually means that one thing follows logically from something else. What is the logical connection between ½ of 6 and ¼ of 8? There isn't any. No logic.

Here is a third question from the same page of the same test as the preceding one:

Different melons weighed 12 lb, 10 lb, 22 lb, 15 lb, and 16 lb. How many pounds did the middle-sized one weigh?

Before answering the question, think of a cantaloupe or honeydew melon in a supermarket: What does it weigh? A small one, 2 or 3 pounds; a big one, 7 or 8 pounds. The question says "12 lb, 10 lb, 22 lb, 15 lb, and 16 lb." Good grief, they are all huge! None of them is middle-sized. They are unreal. No reality.

No sense, no logic, no reality. That is the impression you get from reading through test after standardized test. At first you think there must be some mistake, some one or two test makers who do a particularly poor job. And some tests *are* truly terrible. But *all* of them I have read are at least bad.

Test makers clearly live in some sort of fantasy world. That would be all right by me except that my children and yours are judged by their standards. In order to succeed on these important tests, our children must adopt their crazy logic and distorted view of reality.

From the outside, the testing business seems useful, helpful, normal, and impressive. Most people want to know how well their children are doing in school and how well their school is doing in comparison with other schools. Each test has been tried out with thousands of children ("standardized") so one expects that all the bugs have been worked out of it.

But the tests themselves are secret, in the sense that parents and other public groups cannot examine and discuss them. And as soon as you look *inside* the tests, you realize that instead of being useful, helpful, normal, and impressive, they are none of the above. One feels like Alice in *Through the Looking Glass*, who stepped into the fantasy world behind the mirror over her fireplace.

Then she began looking about, and noticed that what could be seen from the old room was quite common and uninteresting, but that all the rest was as different as possible. For instance, the pictures on the wall next the fire seemed to be all alive, and the very clock on the chimney-piece (you know you can only see the back of it in the Looking Glass) had got the face of a little old man, and grinned at her.

In this chapter we take a very brief stroll around the looking-glass world of standardized achievement tests. (Achievement tests examine what you know or do, as opposed to aptitude or intelligence tests which examine—supposedly—what your potential for learning is.) To keep the story simple, we will quote examples only from tests for elementary and junior high school students (for children up to age 13 or 14).

As you look at one of these test questions, do not congratulate yourself for knowing the "right" answer: that is to be trapped behind the looking glass. Instead, think about the logic and reality of the question itself, the number of different ways it can be interpreted by children from a variety of backgrounds, how many of the given multiple-choice answers could be correct, and where a child must look out for a trick, a trap, or a simple mistake by the test maker.

Two of the questions that began this chapter are examples of looking-glass arithmetic: the manipulation of numbers. But numbers themselves become weirdly distorted in standardized tests. Try this question:

How many hundreds are in 20 tens?

Never mind the answer itself: What possible *use* will the answer have? Does any scientist, doctor, lawyer, shopkeeper, or homeowner need to know how to answer this question? The test maker will mention something about "place value," which means that children should realize that 20 + 1 equals 21 and not 30. But if children have this kind of trouble, you help them with that rather than teach them some jargon.

Apart from its uselessness, the question contains a linguistic trap. Since 20 tens equal 200, therefore there are two hundreds in 20 tens. So the answer is 200, right? Wrong! But never mind.

Here is another question about numbers, in fact the number zero.

36   Which of these are names for zero?

I.   0 + 10
II.   0 x 10
III. 0 ÷ 10
A.   II only
B.   I and II only
C.   II and III only
D.   I, II and III

First of all, what does "names for zero" mean? I know four names for zero: *null, void, zip,* and *zilch.* None of them appears among the answers, so try again. Apparently 0 x 10 is a name for zero. This name for zero is *called* Roman numeral II. Another name for zero is *called* III. The *answer* is "II and III." This answer is *called* letter C. In order to answer the question the poor child has to keep in mind simultaneously all these names

and names for names. He or she may feel like Alice when the White Knight explains the names for his song:

"The name of the song is called '*Haddocks' Eyes.*'"

"Oh, that's the name of the song, is it?" Alice said, trying to feel interested.

The Original Looking-Glass Achievement Test

"Can you do Addition?" the White Queen asked. "What's one and one and one and one and one and one and one and one and one and one?"

"I don't know," said Alice. "I lost count."

"She ca'n't do Addition," the Red Queen interrupted. "Can you do Subtraction? Take nine from eight."

"Nine from eight, I ca'n't, you know," Alice replied readily, "but—"

"She ca'n't do Subtraction," said the White Queen. "Can you do Division? Divide a loaf by a knife—what's the answer to *that*?"

"I suppose—" Alice was beginning, but the Red Queen answered for her. "Bread and Butter, of course. Try another Subtraction sum. Take a bone from a dog: what remains?"

Alice considered. "The bone wouldn't remain, of course, if I took it—and the dog wouldn't remain: it would come to bite me—and I'm sure *I* shouldn't remain!"

"Then you think nothing would remain?" said the Red Queen.

"I think that's the answer."

"Wrong, as usual," said the Red Queen. "The dog's temper would remain."

"But I don't see how—"

"Why, look here!" the Red Queen cried. "The dog would lose its temper, wouldn't it?"

Perhaps it would," Alice replied cautiously.

"Then if the dog went away, its temper would remain!" the Queen exclaimed triumphantly.

Alice said as gravely as she could, "They might go different ways." But she couldn't help thinking to herself, "What dreadful nonsense we are talking!"

"She ca'n't do sums a bit!" the Queens said together, with great emphasis.

"No, you don't understand," the Knight said, looking a little vexed. "That's what the name is *called.* The name really is '*The Aged, Aged Man.*'"

"Then I ought to have said, 'That's what the *song* is called'?" Alice corrected herself.

"No, you oughtn't; that's quite another thing! The *song* is called '*Ways and Means*'; but that's only what it's *called,* you know!"

"Well, what *is* the song, then?" said Alice, who was by this time completely bewildered.

"I was coming to that," the Knight said. "The song really *is* '*A-sitting on a Gate*'; and the tune's my own invention."

Here is an example of what my colleague Judah Schwartz calls "A is to B as C is to almost anything":

Pullman was to railway cars what—
    Whitney was to oil
    Goodyear was to rubber
    Jefferson was to cotton
    Boston was to beans
    don't know

Since there is no unique relationship between different *kinds* of things (such as a person and a product), the item asks, in effect, "What am I thinking?" The result is to penalize inventiveness. Boston produced beans just as surely as Pullman produced railway cars. Tests are full of this kind of question, particularly the college entrance examinations.

In no field is the unreality of the test maker's world more apparent than in science. Here is a looking-glass question about mirrors:

What does this picture of a boy looking at himself in a mirror illustrate?
    —focusing
    —transparency
    —dispersion
    —reflection
    —[don't know]

This is one of many, many examples of a multiple-choice problem in which *all* the choices are correct. The picture of a boy looking at himself in a mirror illustrates focusing on his eyes (and ours!); it illustrates transparency of the glass; it illustrates color fringes due to different speeds of light of different wave-lengths in the glass (called dispersion—the original figure is two-color with blue and black, so is "in color"); and it certainly illustrates reflection. If I cannot choose one among these correct answers, will I be given full credit for choosing the answer "don't know"?

Along with "content," the enterprise of science itself as pictured in achievement tests is seriously distorted. One example began this article. Here is another one:

Which method is used by scientists to discover new facts?

    talking and listening
    reading and writing
    revising and amending
    experimenting and observing

What does *facts* mean? Experimental data? Then clearly "experimenting and observing" is the correct answer. But experimental data are not "discovered" as some kind of surprise: They are recorded as the result of planned experiments. Maybe "new facts" means "new theories." New theories *can* be discovered, but *how* are they discovered? Under what circumstances have *you* had new ideas? While talking or listening or reading or writing or revising or amending or experimenting or observing? Yes! And while dozing or waking or sitting or walking or bicycling or. . . . In truth, this question seriously misrepresents the enterprise of science. In order to answer the question at all, the child must adopt the fantasy world of the test maker.

Are all test items as bad as the ones we have shown? No, but a significant percentage are, the percentage being greater or smaller depending on how you set your sights. Banesh Hoffmann, author of *The Tyranny of Testing,* has a standing offer for test publishers: On any standardized achievement test not concerned merely with trivial facts or routine arithmetical operations, he guarantees that reasonable people will agree that at least 10 percent of the questions are seriously faulty.

He is clearly being conservative: It should not be difficult to find significant faults with 20 percent of standardized test items. Indeed, if one is allowed to object on principle to crowded graphic layout, a separate answer sheet, or the multiple-choice format itself, then the failure rate for test

14

questions themselves can approach 100 percent. But even if only 10 percent are faulty, this constitutes a serious indictment of these tests, since a variation of 10 percent in number of "correct" answers can oftentimes determine whether a child is placed at the top or in the middle of his or her "reference group."

Why are achievement tests so bad? I believe that the primary reason is the test maker's goal of lining up children along a single line by asking, "Who has the higher score?" The inhumane notion that people can and should be compared with one another along a line is the fundamental error that leads to the looking-glass world of testing and its perversion of our educational system.

This notion also leads to the brainless use of statistics in the development of tests. The standardized test is constructed initially by selecting questions from a large reservoir composed by "item writers." The preliminary version is then tried out with different groups of children, each group large enough to provide "statistically significant" information on whether or not each test item discriminates between children in the way that the test makers wish to discriminate. Typically, a revision of the test is tried out with a large selection of children in order to "standardize" the results for different groups.

The test items that survive this selection process are those that make the "appropriate" discriminations between children and not necessarily those that are logical, correct, or clearly laid out, or that actually test the skills that society holds to be important.

This entire process of test development can in principle take place without any child's sitting down with a sensitive adult to try out the questions and discuss which of the difficulties are important and relevant and which are trivial, irrelevant, or caused by the form or layout of the test itself. Until test makers get a lot closer to real individual children, the children who take their tests have the terrible choice between remaining real (and failing) and becoming part of the test maker's dream (and losing their own reality).

If we know how tests come to *be* as bad as they are, why do they *remain* so bad? I believe that the answer is summarized in one word: *secrecy*. So much time and effort go into trying out each test item with large numbers of children that it becomes a valuable property in its own right. To

make such an item public is to destroy its power to compare children with one another. The result is that parents as a group cannot see the tests by which their children are judged. Until parents and teachers can compare notes and seek advice on tests exposed to the light of day, there will be no opportunity for their natural outrage to lead to tests improved in content, humaneness, and connection to the real world.

What shall we make of all this? Shall we laugh or shall we cry? In our outrage shall we demand an end to all achievement testing? Some parents, teachers organizations, and school boards may decide so, and their choice should be respected. Others will continue to feel that children and teachers need to know how well they are doing and that schools need to report to parents and other taxpayers how well children have mastered the skills that society thinks essential to its proper operation. In order to do this task humanely, test development and use must be altered fundamentally.

The first and essential step is to stop comparing one child with other children (so-called "norm-referencing") and instead to try determining whether a child performs the necessary tasks well enough ("criterion referencing"). The best example from the adult world is the automobile driver's test: The driving skills you are expected to demonstrate are not secret, and you either do well enough now or you have to try again later.

Second, test developers must sit down with children individually, watch them take the test, and talk with them afterward about which questions were clear and important and which were confusing or demeaning. The children who try out the tests must be from diverse ethnic and cultural backgrounds, both because tests must not discriminate on these bases and also because all children will benefit from the use of tests that are made understandable for as wide a variety of children as possible.

Third, the usefulness of tests must be judged by how soon after completion children and teachers know which answers are in error and what misunderstandings may have resulted in a given incorrect answer.

Fourth, for tests of "practical skills" such as classifying, describing, narrating, measuring, estimating, graphing, mapping, and doing word problems, test makers must show that performance on the test compares with ability to carry out similar tasks in settings as near to real life as possible.

Finally, when skills can be clearly related to test performance, parents, teachers, and administrators must speak for society by deciding what level of performance on each test shall be called "good enough." As a check on this process, tests must be made public, at least after they have been given locally.

It's a long road back through the looking glass, but some of us are starting down it.

THE WAY IT IS
by Charlotte Darehshori

One of the main goals of education is to implement humanistic programs in our schools. Yet incorporated in these programs as one of the evaluative tools is one of the most dehumanizing practices in education—standardized testing.

While most of us talk in terms of individualized approaches, we employ tests that are constructed to compare child with child, class with class, and school with school. We use tests that not only give us a basis for comparing children, but are purposefully built to "fail" a certain percentage of them.

We tell parents not to compare their child with peers or siblings because this could be damaging to the child's self-concept; we tell children not to compare themselves with others. How then can we justify our practice of using standardized tests that make just such comparisons?

As a teacher, I have found it harder and harder to justify standardized testing philosophically, but it is even more difficult to justify the cruelty of subjecting young children to the act of testing itself.

In giving standardized tests we place children in positions over which they have no control, then we direct them to perform illogical tasks and to act as if everything were perfectly logical.

Taking a standardized test is a bizarre experience for beginning first grade students. Its scenario comes complete with written parts for both teacher and student. For the first time in the children's school careers—perhaps in their lives—they are interacting with an adult who is reading from a script that dictates what, how, and when he or she will react to them. In this play, which is only too real (its results will follow the children throughout their school careers and influence the way some people think of them), all human needs are put aside when the children and the teacher step into their roles.

The children have had virtually no practice for their role. The teacher, in contrast, carries the script around and reads from it word for word.

Going through this performance begins a dehumanizing process for student and teacher alike: Witness this typical testing scene in a first grade classroom in September 1975.

Meet Melanie, a first grader. She is bright, somewhat shy, but loves school. She has begun to make friends, participates in class activities, and seems to be starting a successful school career.

About the third week of school comes testing day. Melanie walks into her room, where the desks have been pushed apart and placed in straight rows to prevent the children from seeing each other's papers.

She sits at her desk. The teacher gives each child a test and a Number 2 pencil and tells the children to work on their own. If they don't know an answer, they are to mark the one they think is best. The test begins.

Melanie has no misgivings about this test. Her teacher has never placed her in a failing situation, so she trusts her completely.

The first item on the test has a picture of a tub. The teacher reads, "Find the letter that has the sound you hear at the end of *tub.*"

Melanie begins to feel uneasy. The test looks different from the practice test she had yesterday. There are lots more funny looking letters and arrows and bubbles to mark in.

"Find the letter that has the sound you hear at the end of *tub,*" the teacher says again.

Just as Melanie starts to become frightened, she sees that one of the letters has already been marked in.

The teacher reads, "Look at the picture of the *stamp* on the other side of the page. This time listen to the sound you hear at the beginning of *stamp.*"

Melanie sees a picture of a stamp. Beside it are three arrows with bubbles. An *st* is beside one of the bubbles; a *cl,* beside another; and a *bl,* beside the last.

Her stomach begins to feel funny; she holds the pencil more tightly.

The teacher goes on, "You should have marked the *s-t*. You hear the sound that *s-t* makes at the beginning of *stamp*. You do not hear *c-l* or *b-l*. You should not have marked these."

The teacher's aide is walking around the room looking at papers. She comes to Melanie. "Melanie, do you understand how to mark your answers?"

Melanie looks up at the aide. "I know I'm supposed to mark in one of these circles. We did that yesterday, but I can't tell which one to mark."

"Just take a good guess and go on."

"But, I don't know, I can't read yet."

The aide pats her on the shoulder, "Just do the best you can."

The teacher goes on, "We are ready to begin. If you do not understand what you are to do, raise your hand. If you are not sure of an answer, mark the one that you think is right. If you change your answer, erase the wrong one. If you want me to repeat any question, raise your hand."

By this time, Melanie and most of the other children are so confused by the maze of instructions, they can't even formulate a question.

Since no one raises a hand, the teacher continues, "First we are going to listen for sounds, at the end of words. Is everyone ready for Number 1? Look at the picture of the *drum*. . . . Mark your answer."

Melanie stares at her paper. She doesn't know what the teacher is asking her to do. She looks around, feeling panic. Since many of the children now have their hands up, she puts hers up. The aide finishes with one of the other children and comes to her side. "I don't know what to do," Melanie whispers, tears in her eyes. The aide can only repeat what the teacher has said.

The teacher goes through 21 more items, including ones in which the children have to be able to distinguish between *e*, *u*, and *i* as the sound heard in the middle of *first*, and *u*, *o*, or *e* as the sound heard in the middle of *rug*.

Everyone greets recess with cheers. The children are exhausted; the aide and the teacher are exhausted.

After recess, the children come back into class and see the test booklets still on their desks. They groan and protest. The teacher gets them settled down and begins the routine again.

In a situation like the one above, the children tend to feel that they are failures; they never suspect that something may be wrong with the test. The teacher, too, is a victim in this testing process, because he or she is made to feel that any problem in carrying out the test is caused by the way he or she has administered it. According to the testing manual, "the teacher or examiner who makes the announcement should guard against arousing anxiety in the students."

During testing week some children remove themselves from the intolerable situation by either "playing sick" or actually becoming sick.

On the second day of testing, Melanie did not want to come to school, but her mother felt it was important for her to go and "not get in the habit of staying home just because something she didn't like was happening." In this way Melanie's mother, like many other parents, helped to support the practice of testing, feeling that it is a necessary evil. The parent thus joins with the school in further convincing the child that something is wrong with the child, not with the test.

Melanie, however, had an asthma attack during the math portion of this test and got to go home anyway. During the rest of the year, she was frequently absent and very reluctant to try new tasks.

In the second grade, the same pattern continued. Melanie's experiences with testing seem to have changed what started as a positive school experience into a negative one.

Unfortunately, this student is not unique. Two or three days of testing frequently damage the self-esteem of many first graders. It is hard to overstate the negative impact of this test on young children.

Other children deal with standardized testing by not really trying, by just marking answers and going through the motions. On the reading comprehension part of the test given above, the children were required to read sentences such as "The prince took a drink and changed into a frog." Only two children in this class were able to read at all.

The children were given 15 minutes for this part of the test. Most went through it marking any bubble that struck their fancy and finished the test in two or three minutes. Some made nice designs with the bubbles. Only the two little boys who could read took more than five minutes for the test. One of them became frustrated because the teacher wouldn't help him with a word, so he put his head down on his desk and refused to finish the test.

The effects of tests on children are tragic and cruel. The vicious cycle of labeling and testing follows children throughout their school experiences, influencing both teacher and parental attitudes toward them—and, what is worse, their attitudes toward themselves.

Much has been written about the effects of testing on teachers' attitudes toward students. We must now contend with a third party in this unhealthy situation. Federal and state programs require increased parent participation, so parents have access to information which they might not otherwise be aware of.

Usually parents whose child has low scores believe either the child or the school is failing.

Teachers who know the limitations of these scores are reluctant to tell parents a first or second grade child is ranked "below average." Providing this information to the parent only perpetuates the labeling of young children. We must question, however, any use whatsoever of a score that is so tainted that we wish to withhold it from a child's parents. If a score is that misleading and damaging in its effects, we must examine the wisdom of even having it available.

We must also question the educational soundness of writing objectives based on raising scores on standardized tests. Suppose a school gets government money for a program to bring all students' scores that are in the lower two quartiles up to the upper two. The tests are constructed, however, to obtain a certain distribution of scores among all four quartiles. The two lower quartiles will by definition always contain a certain proportion of students' scores, so the programs are destined to fall short of their objectives.

It is difficult for a teacher to have worked hard all year only to get the results of standardized tests and find that, technically, the teacher and class both have failed. This year nearly every child in our school is in the lower two quartiles in reading or math or both. Since the main goal of the program at our school is to bring these children into the two top quartiles, the program has failed.

The teachers and staff of our school can accept this failure intellectually because we feel it is only a "paper failure." Emotionally, however, we become frustrated when faced with a list of scores that says our students are failing academically.

These tests also negatively affect the programs that they evaluate. In schools where the staff is professional and secure, the influence of these tests is minimal as the staff tries to keep the children's needs in mind and teach to these needs, not to the tests. Even so, the need to compare skills achievement with that in other schools gives the tests influence. Because evaluation techniques and standardized tests have not kept pace with curriculum development and theories of child development, that influence is regressive.

In other schools, the situation is worse. At one school where I taught, great emphasis was placed on the test results. Predictably, teachers did everything possible to improve the test scores. Since the only two areas evaluated on the test were math and reading, teachers concentrated on these two areas almost to the exclusion of art, social studies, and music. Recess and lunch time were cut down in order to give more instructional time in math and reading. Testing was manipulated to make the pretest scores lower than the posttest scores. For pretesting, all the tests were given in one day, on a Monday; for posttesting, they were given at a more leisurely pace on Tuesday, Wednesday, and Thursday—days when the children were usually more settled.

Tests and work sheets covering the material on the test finally came to be the curriculum at the school. The pressure to look good on tests brought about wide fluctuations in students' test scores—gains of two or three years one year and regression the next.

It seems, then, that little of value is derived from these tests, other than using the scores as criteria for deciding which schools will get federal money for new programs. (Why not throw darts?)

To student, teacher, and parent, the tests are equally devastating. One teacher at William Penn Elementary School (Bakersfield, California) put it very succinctly, "How do standardized tests help me in the classroom? Well, they helped three children ruin their pants and one child have an asthma attack."

Teachers have talked about the damaging effects of standardized tests for years. Perhaps if they refused to give the tests, changes and reforms would result.

One immediate change could be to exclude children from standardized testing until they actually have the skills that these tests are supposed to be testing. Teachers could use their judgment to decide who should take the tests.

Because these tests are not diagnostic and are supposed to be more valid (although this, too, is questionable) for a group than for an individual, test results should not be linked with an individual student but only with a group.

On a long-term basis, test manufacturers should design tests based on the developmental levels of young children—not adults. In curriculum we realized years ago that the child is a unique kind of being and not just a smaller version of a grown-up. Merely updating the old model of the standardized test as testing companies have done in the past and continue to do is not enough.

ONE WAY IT CAN BE
by Brenda S. Engel

Until the spring of 1976, the Cambridge Alternative Public School, then in its fourth year, had generally avoided administering the standardized tests ordinarily required of Cambridge public schools. At that time, however, pressure from the school department was increasing; the assistant superintendent for elementary education felt that he needed concrete evidence of the quality of the education offered at the school.

With parent support, the school had taken an antitesting position (similar, on several points, to that taken by the NEA). The school felt that scheduling standardized tests disrupted the educational process, that the tests made many children anxious, that the tests penalized minority children, and that their influence on teaching and the curriculum could be disastrous for an innovative school. But the school community (teachers, administration, and parents) also had a strong interest in carrying out some form of evaluation in order to corroborate their confidence in the school. So much for the situation.

At this point, at the request of a parent-staff committee, I was employed as an independent consultant to try out some means of evaluation that might be satisfactory to both the school community and the school department.

We settled on the third grade for the alternative evaluation, because it was a well-balanced class in regard to age, sex, and race. Four teachers would be directly involved since the 29 children in the grade were fairly evenly divided among four classrooms (each contained mixed ages). Most of the children involved had been in the school from its inception.

In order to keep the size of the undertaking manageable during the first experimental year, we identified three areas of the curriculum for assessment—math, reading, and art—and proceeded to make an overall plan, to outline an implementation schedule, and to design the actual instruments of evaluation.

The evaluation was to be carried out over a five-week period toward the end of the school year. We hoped the instruments of evaluation would do the following:

- Give each child various ways to demonstrate his or her abilities.
- Take into consideration the varied economic, cultural, and linguistic backgrounds of the children.
- Elicit original responses and creative thinking.
- Assess significant aspects of education.
- Gain information about children's learning as directly as possible.

We also hoped that the evaluation would cause a minimum of disruption in the school and that it would not be a negative experience for the children. The actual work of the assessment was to be shared among a number of people with different jobs in the school or with different relationships to it.

When the evaluation was completed, we hoped to present a report in clear, readable, and usable form. We planned to make it more descriptive than judgmental, both noncomparative and nonnumerical, and useful to teachers as well as informative to administrators and parents.

The matrix shown in Figure 1 describes *what* we intended to assess and *how* we intended to do it. The Areas to Be Assessed are listed across the top and the Means of Assessment down the left-hand side. Teacher statements led the list of Means of Assessment. Each teacher gave opinions (which we determined through lengthy interviews) of each child's progress in each area of learning: his or her understanding of the decimal system, sense of estimation and of probability, and so on across the matrix, ending with the child's ability to solve original problems.

The teacher statements began the evaluation process and supplied the guidelines, in both content and approach, for conducting the rest of the assessment. The teachers' opinions of each child's ability in each curriculum area set the stage for

Figure 1

AREAS TO BE ASSESSED

NOTES

✓ indicates means chosen

• indicates possible means

MEANS OF ASSESSMENT \ AREAS OF LEARNING / CHARACTERISTICS OF LEARNING	MATH: decimal system	estimation	probability & statistics	measurements (inc. time)	ratio/mapping	shapes	computation (inc. fractions)	graphic representation	classification & sets	math problem solving	symmetry & balance	feelings towards math	relation of performance to understanding	READING: how much	where (home &/or school)	kinds	feelings about reading	degree of difficulty	understanding, vocabulary	fluency	ART: how much	where (home &/or school)	what kinds	feelings about art	knowledge of techniques	developmental level	originality & imagination	problem solving, autonomous thinking
Teachers' statements	✓	✓	✓	✓	✓	✓	✓	✓	✓	✓	✓	✓	✓	✓	✓	✓	✓	✓	✓	✓	✓		✓	✓	✓	✓	✓	✓
Classroom observations	•	•	•	•	•	•	•	•	•	•	•	✓	•	•		•	✓	•	•	•			•	✓	•	•	•	•
Current questionnaires		✓		✓			✓		✓			✓		✓	✓	✓	✓			✓	✓	✓	✓	✓				✓
Oral tests	✓	✓	✓	✓						✓	✓		✓					✓	✓	✓							•	•
Written tests		✓		✓	✓	✓	✓	✓		✓	✓		✓					✓	✓							✓	•	✓
Evidence, work samples	✓			✓	✓	✓	✓	✓	•				✓	✓		✓	✓	✓	•		✓		✓		✓	✓	✓	✓
Previous test results / School records	✓			✓		✓	✓		•				✓					✓	✓									
Child interviews	•	•	•		•	•	•		•		•	✓	✓	✓	✓	✓	✓	✓	✓	✓	✓	✓	✓	✓	✓			•

22

what followed, particularly for our observations of, and interviews with, the children.

The second Means of Assessment—classroom observations—was necessarily open-ended and directed more toward quality of work and involvement than toward skills. An observer spent about half a day in each of the four classrooms, focusing particularly on the third graders and recording the observations in anecdotal form.

A parent committee drew up and distributed parent questionnaires, the third item in the Means column. The areas checked on the matrix represent only some of the subjects covered in the questionnaires; other subjects were matters of general interest to the school and were not part of the assessment.

The oral and written tests were made up specifically for the occasions (i.e., nonstandardized). They were to inventory the children's abilities in the specified areas as simply as possible.

Following is an example from such a test. It was designed to measure children's ability to estimate as part of the mathematical skills assessed on the matrix.

About how much does your teacher weigh?

Which do you think weighs more, a bicycle or a horse?

About how long is your thumb?

About how high is the ceiling in this room?

About how long does it take you to brush your teeth?

About how long will it be before you are a grown-up?

About how long is summer vacation?

About how many children are there in this school?

About how many pieces of bread are there in a loaf?

Classroom teachers, with the help of graduate students, gathered the next items on the list—collection of work samples (current), previous test results, and summaries of school records.

Finally, when all these data were assembled in folders, we conducted an interview with each child to fill in any gaps in the information and clear up possible ambiguities or contradictions.

Most important, each area of learning was examined in a variety of ways designed to cross-check each other. No judgments were made on the basis of a single means or single occasion.

Another central and challenging consideration was the form of the final report, which had to be designed for the requirements of widely different constituencies: the school department, school administration, teachers, parents, and children.

The school department was interested in a concise statement focused mainly on skills. Parents, although they varied in their expectations of the evaluations (some looking for cognitive; others, affective assessment), were primarily interested in detailed reports on their own children. Teachers were looking for confirmation of their own perceptions, for further insights, and for implications for the curriculum. The school administration shared all these interests. The children themselves, if they were at all aware of the nature of the process, were looking for personal reassurance.

Our reporting system had three parts: a summary sheet for each child, a key (with school department expectations, *not norms*, underlined), and documentation (folders containing results of, or notes on, all the Means of Assessment). By glancing at only the summary sheet, one could gain a general impression of achievement; one could read the summary sheet in detail, using the key to identify specific skills; or one could scrutinize the actual evidence on which the summary sheet was based.

It would be misleading to suggest that all of this does not add up to a substantial amount of work. Having gone through this process once, however, those of us involved now believe that the same approach could be carried out in a variety of ways and over differing lengths of time.

A teacher, or group of teachers, could custom design his or her own matrix, listing the subject matter to be assessed across the top (as shown in Figure 1) and the feasible means of assessment down the lefthand column. The matrix itself, once it has been filled out, can provide the framework for the assessment process. For instance, one might limit the means to teacher statements, parent questionnaires, written tests, and work samples. Similarly, one could limit the areas to be scrutinized. (It is important, however, to assess each area in at least three ways.) Later, then, when the time comes to write a test or plan a questionnaire, one has only to look across the horizontal row from a particular means to identify its content. Classroom teachers can formulate the specific questions to be asked without much difficulty.

After the scheduled information has been collected for each child, the teacher can fill in a report for each child, viewing the assessment as a more-than-adequate substitute for the usual reports and tests—not as an addition to them.

How to assess the assessment in relation to our expectations? At this point, it is important to reemphasize that the purpose of this alternative evaluation was to compile as informative and as comprehensive a picture of each child's abilities and skills as possible—not to compare children's

achievements or rates of growth with those of other children. In this context, the findings have promise.

The children, by their own accounts during their interviews, seemed to enjoy the process, which was neither seriously interruptive nor damaging. With the additional specific information about each student gained from the assessment, teachers felt that they could do a better job of individualizing the educational program for each child. Perhaps most important, the assessment itself did not violate the educational climate we were trying to protect and to which we were committed.

ROLES AND RESPONSIBILITIES OF GROUPS CONCERNED WITH STUDENT EVALUATION SYSTEMS*
by Bernard McKenna

The roles and responsibilities delineated below for specific groups of persons particularly concerned with student evaluation are based on findings of and positions taken by the NEA Task Force on Testing. (The report of this task force is contained on pages 81-90.) These recommended roles and responsibilities are considered essentials for achieving the following goals:

- Sound and fair development of evaluation systems
- Appropriate distribution and administration of evaluation systems
- Accurate and fair interpretation of the results
- Relevant and constructive action programs based on the results.

A. Teachers, Individually or Collectively Through Their Associations, as Appropriate, Should Do the Following:

1. Seek representation on school district, testing industry, and government (state and federal) decision-making groups for test development (e.g., Educational Testing Service, National Institute of Education), become involved in item analysis and selection, and provide feedback on content and format of tests.
2. Plan and negotiate for, or otherwise reach agreement with the school administration on, released time and district in-service education programs to prepare members in the use of tests.
3. Plan professional activities in the area of testing for all members of the association.
4. Seek and participate in in-service training in the area of testing to learn to construct and evaluate teacher-made tests, to learn about objective- or criterion-referencing, to learn about alternative assessment tools, to learn appropriate reporting procedures, to develop an awareness of the variety of tests and their pur-

poses, to keep abreast of latest research findings, and to develop the ability to analyze and criticize standardized tests as they relate to school and district programs and goals.
5. Work to influence test makers and the local and state school systems and secure from them a firm commitment to evaluation programs that will lead to the improvement of instruction.
6. Keep parents and other interested community groups informed about trends and promising developments in evaluation procedures and about unsound testing practices.
7. Negotiate for, or otherwise reach agreement with the school administration on, provisions guaranteeing teacher lead time for preparation for testing, appropriate testing conditions and scheduling, and follow-up time for scoring. Provisions should spell out teachers' appropriate role in the test-scoring process, e.g., to remedy the inordinate amount of time spent on hand scoring.
8. Thoroughly familiarize themselves with tests to be given (assuming they have been furnished with appropriate background materials and sufficient time for learning about administration of the instruments).
9. Develop an understanding of their students' cultural and socio-economic backgrounds and sensitivity to their individual needs and problems in order to avoid the possibility of irrelevant and biased testing.
10. Periodically review tests to determine their relevancy to instructional goals and objectives and their timeliness, and

---

*The term *evaluation systems* is used instead of *tests* because it is believed that a wide variety of alternatives to tests should and can be developed through research and tryout leading to their validation for evaluation purposes.

recommend to the school administration and the testing industry abandonment of irrelevant and outmoded tests.

11. Secure by appropriate means—from the school or school district administration, as deemed necessary—the right to determine what tests will be administered, when they will be given, and at what intervals. They should also secure the right to determine exemptions from testing.

12. Secure by appropriate means—from the school or school district administration, as deemed necessary—the right to determine proper physical arrangements and time frames for testing as appropriate for themselves and their students. Time allowed should be sufficient for thorough orientation of students to the test being given, and for scoring and reporting results.

13. Be responsible for providing a non-threatening attitudinal atmosphere for students during testing sessions, given the proper conditions.

14. Assure that machine-scored results are validated by hand scoring a sample of tests.

15. Take an objective approach in interpreting test results, never using them as a weapon against students.

16. Seek to ensure that test results are not used to categorize students into homogeneous groups or as a criterion for student admission to programs of their choice.

17. Strive for accuracy in interpreting test results, relating them to socio-economic factors affecting individual students.

18. Have respect for student privacy in interpreting test results and manifest that respect by working to secure school district policies guaranteeing students' privacy in the reporting and dissemination of test results, which should not be for public information.

19. Urge strict enforcement of the federal Privacy Act affecting pupil records.

20. Work to secure legislation which will prevent publication of test scores.

21. Work to secure legislation which will prevent the use of test results as a basis for allocation of local, state, or federal educational funding.

22. Assure that test results are not compared among classrooms or buildings or with other districts or regions.

23. Report on test results in a manner appropriate to a varied audience—students, parents, media, professionals.

24. Recommend general and specific program improvements to the school and school district administrations, and to effect the improvements, identify the needed resources and remedial measures and programs.

25. Secure through the appropriate means—from the school or school district administration, as deemed necessary—the stipulation that test results will not be used in evaluating teacher performance. (Teachers should be held accountable for conducting the best instructional process possible under existing conditions, not for guaranteeing learning.)

26. Take a position in favor of the inclusion of courses in tests and measurements in all teacher preparation programs, and provide input on testing problems and issues to their representatives on professional governance boards or commissions to help in the formulation of standards and requirements for teacher education and licensure. (There is little evidence that most preparing institutions or states specifically require or encourage classroom teachers to acquire the knowledge and skills necessary for using tests.)

B. Other Professional Associations Should Do the Following:

1. Search out and synthesize information on all issues associated with the development, use, and abuse of tests and communicate to the members any information affecting them or their students.

2. Organize study committees of members knowledgeable in testing to develop policies, guidelines, and procedures for testing. Such committees should seek in-

put from all members and consultation from experts in the field.

3. Serve in a "watchdog" capacity on the introduction and administration of curriculum-related tests to assure their appropriateness for schools, and communicate regional concerns to the testing industry.

4. Pursue needed changes in school curriculum programs as identified through the results of testing, this in cooperation with other associations in the region which represent comparable educational and socioeconomic conditions.

5. Identify alternatives to standardized testing.

6. Provide background information and regional concerns to those responsible for drafting or introducing state legislation, and work for passage of legislation to regulate types of tests and uses of the results. These efforts should include calling for the testing of students in their dominant language (except, for example, proficiency tests in English).

7. Urge strict enforcement of the federal Privacy Act affecting pupil records.

C. Students, Individually or Collectively as Appropriate, Should Do the Following:

1. Seek a role in the development of tests through representation on school, district, and testing industry committees and by providing feedback on test content and format.

2. Take positions against the use of measurement instruments that they feel are biased and will lead to unfair results on the basis of race, sex, socioeconomic status, language, or culture, and make these positions known to the school and school district administration and the testing industry.

3. Make every effort, assuming they have been afforded proper orientation, to thoroughly understand the purpose, and intended uses of results, of any test to be administered in which they will be involved. Students should have the right to refuse to take a test known to be racially, culturally, or otherwise biased.

4. Seek a role in determining the conditions of test administration—including scheduling, preparation, length, location, facilities. (Many tests are administered under adverse conditions, with little attention given to the total physical environment and insufficient time allowed for orientation.)

5. Call attention to any physical or attitudinal pressures in the administration of tests which they feel threaten them or their performance.

6. Insist that they be given a thorough explanation of test results in a meaningful way and in language they can understand.

7. Take a position on the use of test results, demanding guarantees of privacy and the right to determine to whom the results will be released, insisting that results not be used to demean or categorize them or to deny them admission to programs of their choice, and urging strict enforcement of the federal Privacy Act which affects pupil records.

8. Seek a role in deciding on alternatives for meeting student needs as identified through the results of testing, insist on the right to choose from among alternatives, and become involved in the planning of remedial programs.

Local Student Action for Education and Student NEA groups might assume the leadership role in involving all students in the evaluation programs of the school or school district and serve as the voice of student opinion and the vehicle for their protection against the adverse effects of evaluation.

D. Minority Groups Should Do the Following:

1. Actively seek representative involvement on testing industry and school system decision-making groups for test development and use.

2. Urge test makers to (a) revise tests in consideration of minority differences, eliminating culture-related items from

current tests and working toward cross-cultural instruments, (b) research ethnic and regional test requirements and withdraw tests found to be inappropriate to the population being tested, and (c) explore and recommend alternative forms of student evaluation.

3. Request from the testing industry documentation on norming procedures and population bases for norming.

4. Keep members informed of improper test procedures and seek support or legal assistance where tests and results are misused.

5. Urge minority students to refuse to take tests which are found to be biased and urge minority teachers to refuse to administer such tests.

6. Work to prevent the invasion of student privacy in interpretation and use of test results.

7. Work for legislation to prevent publication of test scores and for enforcement of the federal Privacy Act affecting pupil records.

8. Promote legislation to prevent the use of test scores as a basis for allocation of local, state, or federal educational funding.

9. Take strong positions and action against the use of test results for tracking, to denigrate minority intelligence, or to deny students entrance to programs.

10. Expose the erroneous contentions of Shockley and Jensen that some groups in society are genetically less intelligent than others. (The typical group test is considered (a) an unreliable measure of mental ability and (b) to be biased against minorities, having been standardized on a different kind of population.)

11. Actively seek changes in curriculum (including textbooks) to reflect minority concerns and diagnostic services based on student needs as identified by appropriate testing.

12. Seek community support and funds for appropriate new or experimental education programs based on needs identified through means other than testing.

13. Become involved in planning and providing pre- and in-service education for teachers to orient them to minority problems and needs related to testing.

14. Seek public awareness of and concern for minority problems in testing, and pressure community media to help keep the public informed, especially on issues related to proper interpretation and use of test results.

15. Form coalitions for action in the development and use of tests.

E. The Testing Industry Should Do the Following:

1. Include in test development substantial numbers of persons from all groups that have an interest in and knowledge about testing, particularly representatives of classroom teachers and minority groups.

2. Be responsible for producing culturally fair and bias-free tests that contain relevant items.

3. Work with all concerned groups in constantly monitoring, updating, and revising their tests. The industry should immediately withdraw out-of-date tests from the market, as recommended by those who use them.

4. Take regional diversities into consideration in constructing tests to ensure relevance of test items.

5. Correlate tests to current and developing curricula.

6. Improve sampling techniques and broaden sampling bases.

7. Undertake in-depth research and development to perfect a wide variety of alternatives to standardized norm-referenced tests.

8. Provide with each test copy a cover document specifying what the test is designed for (to reveal depth of subject knowledge, to verify reading comprehension, to establish equivalency, etc.) and what groups (e.g., "early childhood," "later elementary") it is appropriate for. The document should also include a release form for student signature testifying that "I understand the purpose of

28

the test. . .” or “I am taking test under protest. . . .”

9. Provide an up-to-date manual with each standardized test, issued in English and other appropriate language editions depending on the student population. The manual should give clear and complete information for administration of the test, including proper physical arrangements; define proper and improper uses of the test, warning particularly against using the test for purposes of teacher evaluation; explain various ways of interpreting results, providing information on the basis of norming to ensure proper interpretation and including a “Surgeon General’s warning” on the dangers of misinterpretation; delineate limitations of the test.

10. Provide with each test, not just bench marks, but a range of scoring norms.

11. Constantly monitor the distribution of standardized tests to ensure proper use, respond promptly to charges of misuse, and refuse to sell tests or report scores where misuse is evident.

12. Provide in-service training for teachers and administrators in the use of standardized tests; provide consultants and test administrators to assist teachers in giving tests and developing sensitivity to testing conditions; and have representatives available as resource persons for interpretation of test results.

13. Provide information on the use of standardized tests and interpretation of results to schools of education and urge them to include courses in tests and measurements in their required professional preparation for teachers. Such courses should include instruction on limitations of tests, potential bias, and a broad range of alternatives to testing.

14. Develop recommendations for curriculum revisions as related to test results in order to help teachers in planning remedial programs for students.

15. Establish an extensive PR program to keep the public informed on testing issues and developments, issuing information materials in English and other language editions.

F. School Administrators Should Do the Following:

1. Ensure that, when appropriate, all tests to be administered reflect the uniqueness of the geographic region in which they are administered and that locally developed and standardized tests reflect updated curriculum.

2. Involve teachers, students, and parents in decision making related to the testing program.

3. Ensure that all teachers who must administer tests are provided with adequate supplies for the students, proper physical arrangements, and thorough orientation time, including practice testing.

4. Provide released time for teachers for in-service training in the administration of tests.

5. Ensure that test results are not used to label students, that the confidentiality of scores is protected in a professional manner, and that the federal Privacy Act affecting pupil records is enforced in school buildings and districts.

6. Make available to teachers or specialists tools for diagnostic purposes and training in their use.

7. Keep parents informed about test results (using nontechnical language) and keep the school board informed about the limitations and possible misuses of tests.

8. Continually evaluate the total testing program.

G. Appropriate College and University Personnel Should Do the Following:

1. Serve a research function, providing to NEA and other concerned groups and to faculty in the school of education their findings on the use and misuses of standardized tests (including their own testing devices), test bias, and alternatives.

2. Serve in a consultative capacity to the testing industry, providing information on student population and needs, new

curricula, college admission policies, scholarships, equal opportunity programs, and the like.

3. Serve in a consultative capacity to school systems for in-service teacher education and for decision making about curriculum changes based on the results of testing.

4. Seek the involvement of practitioners in decision making, relating to professional preparation in tests and measurements.

5. Monitor test results from school districts in their region in relation to new directions for open admissions, equal opportunity programs, scholarships, etc., and keep junior and senior high schools informed about the relationship of test scores to admission policies and program choice.

6. Form coalitions to influence legislation and provide expert testimony on the proper uses of tests and test results.

H. Government Agencies

1. The U.S. Congress should legislate restraints on the use of tests that prevent equal educational opportunity.

2. The approriate federal agencies should—
   - Provide quality control of testing by taking steps to restrain the testing industry from publishing tests that are improperly constructed and by monitoring instruments to ensure their constant updating.
   - Provide technical assistance and information to educators and the public regarding test development and use.
   - Increase research efforts in standardized tests and alternatives.
   - Assure that teachers are involved in decision making about the use of revenue-sharing funds as they apply to the school system's testing program.

3. State education agencies should—
   - Provide consultant services, financial assistance, and models for quality in-service education for teachers on the proper administration of tests and on limitations of test results.
   - Provide for alternatives to standardized tests for state assessment programs.
   - Prevent the improper distribution and administration of large-scale assessment program materials by instituting sampling procedures as opposed to blanket testing.

4. Local education agencies should—
   - Provide released time and quality in-service education for teachers and other school personnel on the administration of tests and use of results.
   - Prevent misuse of large-scale assessment instruments by instituting sampling procedures as opposed to blanket testing.

5. Education agencies at all levels should—
   - Involve teachers in decision making on test development.
   - Provide the funds for innovative programs to develop alternatives to standardized testing and interpretation.
   - Provide the funds for long-range experimental testing programs.

WHY SHOULD ALL THOSE STUDENTS TAKE ALL THOSE TESTS?

The NEA Task Force on Testing, in its first interim report, states:

> The Task Force believes there is overkill in the use of standardized tests and that the intended purposes of testing can be accomplished through less use of standardized tests, through sampling techniques where tests are used, and through a variety of alternatives to tests. . . .

> Representatives of the testing industry and others told the Task Force that sampling of student populations could be as effective as the blanket application of tests that is now so common. Some suggested that such procedures, in addition to increasing the assurance of privacy rights, would conserve time, effort, and financial expenditure.[1]

The blanket use of tests (every-pupil testing) in some state assessment and local testing programs appears to require inordinate amounts of time and resources on the part of teachers, other personnel involved in test administration and interpretation, and the students themselves.

Criticisms of the blanket use of tests have come from a variety of prominent researchers, evaluators, and other educators.

House, Rivers, and Stufflebeam, in their evaluation of the Michigan accountability system, concurred that in that state:

> Statewide testing as presently executed also raises the question of the feasibility of every pupil testing. This practice appears to be of dubious value when the cost of such an undertaking is compared with the resulting benefits to local level personnel. . . . The local, and hence overall, costs could be reduced by a matrix sampling plan which requires that each student tested take only a few items. . . . In the long run, a matrix sampling plan will be the only one feasible from a cost and time standpoint. The cost and time required for every pupil testing for the whole state would be horrendous. . . . We feel that it [strict adherence to a statewide testing model] will result in useless expenditures of monies and manpower, in addition to producing unwarranted disruptions of the educational programs within a great number of schools.[2]

In a paper entitled "Criteria for Evaluating State Education Accountability Systems," the Na-tional Education Association has laid down fifteen basic principles, one of which is as follows:

> If the state desires test data for its own planning purposes, it should use proven matrix sampling techniques which will not reveal schools and which will greatly reduce costs.

> Matrix sampling techniques can give an accurate picture of the state by various categories much more efficiently than testing each child with an entire instrument.[3]

It was with such admonitions as these in mind that this chapter was written. And while some procedures are appropriate for evaluating all students in one way or another for particular purposes, it would appear that there is gross over-use of blanket testing procedures.

To help teachers and other educators better understand some main considerations related to sampling, the NEA obtained permission from Dr. Frank Womer, Michigan School Testing Service, University of Michigan, to reproduce material from a monograph of his on developing assessment programs.[4] In addition, Dr. Womer prepared, especially for this paper, a section on item sampling. Dr. Womer's recommendations follow the excerpts from his monograph.

* * * * * *

Determining Whether Sampling Is To Be Used

The decision whether to test an entire population or use a sample involves a combination of concerns. Clearly there are policy considerations; clearly there are psychometric[5] considerations; clearly there are data collection considerations; and clearly there are cost considerations. The best possible staff and consultant thinking on this question should be brought to an advisory committee for them to consider very carefully.

Probably the most crucial consideration is a policy one, since psychometrics, data collection, and cost generally would argue on the side of sampling rather than using an entire population. If it is deemed wise for policy reasons to test all students in a population, that preference, typically, will have to be weighed against available resources and technology; so we will consider first the policy implications of the two choices.

One needs to look carefully at the purposes and goals of a specific assessment program in determining whether sampling is appropriate. If all of the specific purposes and objectives of an assessment program can be met by *group* results, then sampling must be considered.

The only assessment situation that clearly calls for common data collection on all members of the population is when it is deemed essential, for improved decision making, to have exactly the same test information for every pupil in a given grade in a state (or other assessment unit). It is exactly this situation that has prevailed for years in local school districts that have every-pupil achievement or ability testing at some grade level. Historically, the compulsory state testing programs were examples of this situation; the voluntary programs were not. If a state mandates common testing for all students it is taking over a role that local districts traditionally have held. This may be good or this may be bad depending on one's point of view of the role of a state department of education. It certainly has important policy implications.

There are many facets to this point, but it should be kept clearly in mind that *it is not necessary to test every pupil at a given grade level on identical material in order to get a good picture of education outcomes* of groups of students; it is necessary only if one feels that *each* teacher in an entire state at a given grade level must have the same information for *each* pupil.

Probably *the greatest advantage of sampling is that for a given amount of effort* (and money) *one can gather more usable information than by using an entire population.* If the goals of an assessment program are to gather statewide information only, it is hard to conceive of any reason for testing all students in a given grade. For example, if there are 50,000 third-graders in the state of Limbo, and one wants to gather state statistics only, it is very possible that a sample 5,000 students (or even 500) would be sufficient if they are selected by a probability sample....[6] Or, if one can afford to test all 50,000 third-graders, and if it is deemed wise to do so, one could select ten 5,000-pupil

samples and secure information on ten subject areas, or one could go into great depth of information gathering in two or three subject areas. The combinations of possibilities of sampling pupils and content are almost endless.

If one wants district-level information, then sampling becomes a different situation. In a school district with one third grade, sampling of pupils is hardly possible for most assessment purposes. In school districts with many third-graders, sampling could provide a greater variety of information than common testing on every pupil, in the same fashion as at the state level. Specific decisions of how far to carry sampling should be made only after advice from a sampling statistician. Sampling is a highly developed technical field, and the implications of any decisions to sample or not to sample must be reviewed by competent samplers.

Other compromise possibilities exist. One could test all students in a population with one short test, while using a sampling approach for other tests. This approach would provide some common information on all students but would allow for greater depth of data collection over a subject area.

> Principle: Sampling of pupils and/or content should be given very serious consideration for all large-scale assessment projects. The only situation where it may not be useful is one where it is deemed essential to collect common information on all students in a statewide population of students. Sampling should be used to maximize the collection of usable information for stated assessment purposes at the lowest possible cost and effort.

* * *

[Sampling with total tests is less complicated to administer, but since it is likely to be subject to error in administration and consequently less reliable, in some cases item sampling may be more useful. Therefore, Dr. Womer was asked to prepare an additional statement on the purposes and potential of item sampling. His statement follows.]

Item Sampling

The process of item sampling in testing is more useful for one of two purposes:

1. To increase the amount of group test results that can be obtained from students in a given period of time, or

32

2. To decrease the amount of testing time necessary to obtain large amounts of group test information from students.

For either purpose, it is essential to keep in mind that item sampling is useful for gathering information about groups of students. Thus it is a technique for use with relatively large groups, not a classroom-sized group or even three or four classes within a building.

Example 1

A school system has 500 students in the sixth grade. A standardized reading test is to be administered for a one-shot systemwide survey. The test takes 45 minutes to administer, which is all the time that can be taken from a busy schedule at the end of the year.

Staff are unhappy that only reading is to be surveyed. Some major changes were made in the mathematics curriculum three years before and they feel it would be valuable to survey this subject also. By randomly selecting only 250 of the students to take the reading test, the other 250 could be given a 45-minute mathematics test at the same time.

Example 2

A school system has 1,000 fourth-graders. It is desired to do an in-depth study of student outcomes for 100 different behavioral objectives in mathematics. Each objective requires the use of eight questions. The total of 800 questions would require one student to spend perhaps 15 hours of testing time to attempt all of them.

By randomly dividing up the objectives and items into five different subtests (each with 20 objectives and 160 items), each subtest could be administered to 200 students (randomly selected). This would require only 3 hours of testing time per student (manageable) rather than 15 hours (unmanageable), and group results would still be available for all 100 objectives (800 items).

In either example the results will be usable for group analyses. Any slight reduction in accuracy due to sampling error is apt to be much less than errors due to increasing testing time of students beyond some reasonable amount. Systematic errors due to fatigue, disinterest, poor motivation, teacher concern, and other conditions of testing can easily outweigh a small sampling error.

A TEACHER VIEWS CRITERION-REFERENCED TESTS
by Jean S. Blachford

Recently, students and teachers have been questioning the use of standardized tests, including their administration, ranking, scoring, and reporting procedures. We teachers deplore the use of tests to rank students and recognize that use of standardized tests does not, in fact, improve educational programs.

In response to these negative reactions, test developers have offered the criterion-referenced test (CRT), which tells something about an individual student without reference to the performance of any other student. Despite this advantage of CRT over norm-referenced tests, we teachers must still consider several things as we become part of the national movement toward criterion-referenced tests. We must also seek relevant and constructive action programs to learn about alternative assessment tools.

Given the CRT methodology, teachers must have assurance that the test items are directly based on the instructional objectives that are included in their students' curriculum. Neither students nor we teachers should be assessed on test items that reflect educational outcomes not included in the local instructional program.

It is important that objectives be developed at the local level and that they take into consideration the fact that all learning cannot be translated into CRT items. Evidence is fast accumulating that cognitive processes are measurable but that higher-level thought processes are very difficult to measure. Thus we find ourselves measuring very simple tasks. As teachers, we must be aware that the test questions directly related to instruction are limited to assessing mastery of specifics and do not assess a student's general ability.

Indeed, if we are permitted to formulate the instructional objectives for our own students, we must use caution in selecting the objectives that meet the personal needs of the particular children we teach. Selection of improper objectives can lead to highly detrimental consequences. Narrowly structured objectives may be readily mastered by students, but they are grossly unfair to students and to the teacher. Those students who are taught only through a set of rigidly applied performance objectives are being denied the broad experience of varied learning styles and creative teaching techniques.

Consider, for example, what might happen if students were required to master in a 10-week period the following seven objectives taken from an elementary item bank in the skill area of language arts comprehension:

1. Retell a story
2. Use a given word in a written sentence
3. Name the class of a group of pictures
4. Identify synonyms
5. Identify antonyms
6. Select a picture to match a sentence
7. Recall facts for *who, what,* and *where* questions.

If students miss the established mastery level, the teacher faces this dilemma: Have they missed by only a little? On the other hand, if students master the objectives in an outstanding manner, the teacher may not know whether their performance indicates a high likelihood of success on subsequent objectives or whether the CRT items were written in such a way that competency was assured.

Two other problems that plague teachers are related to the way criterion-referenced tests are developed and how their results are used.

One is that test items are developed in a hierarchy of difficulty which almost assures that certain percentages of students will not be able to respond correctly to some items. This flies in the face of the very philosophy of instructional objectives: that all students should be helped to achieve all objectives as fully as possible and that a major purpose of testing ought to be to determine which students need more work on which objectives in order that they may achieve full mastery.

The second, which is closely related to the first, is the use of cutting scores, pass-fail points, or minimal competency levels. Reporting and decision making based on such measures can result in the use of criterion-referenced tests for the sorting and classifying of students—a practice that has been found so objectionable with means, quartiles, and similar statistics in norm-referenced tests.

Finally, if we are to pursue CRT as an aid in meeting the instructional needs of our students, we must insist upon proper in-service education in the preparation of test items that are attributable to our instruction. The items must be developed in such a way that each item will require a specific response. We must be thoroughly instructed in sound and fair development of CRT items.

GUIDELINES AND CAUTIONS FOR CONSIDERING CRITERION-REFERENCED TESTING
by Bernard McKenna

Standardized achievement tests used in most schools today are known as norm-referenced tests. They are constructed in such a way as to maximize differences among students so that one can be compared to another. This is done by providing for maximum discrimination between high and low scores. The purpose is to rank a student among his or her peers. Hence, scores are reported in such terms as "Chris Jones is in the ninety-fifth percentile on verbal reasoning." While norm-referenced tests are useful for sorting people into categories (to the dismay of many), they are not useful for improving educational programs.

Recently a new concept has been promoted among test makers and the educational public called "criterion-referenced testing," also termed "objective-referenced testing." At least three factors have contributed to the emergence of this new concept: First, there is a strong and rising dissatisfaction with tests in general; second, there is the inadequacy of traditional tests for diagnostic and instructional purposes; and third, there is some clamor for evaluating instruction and teachers as part of the accountability movement. Although criterion or objective-referenced tests may have potential for diagnosing learning problems and improving instruction, they are not useful for evaluating teachers. For test scores depend largely on variables in a student's background rather than on what he or she is taught in the classroom. Even so, a few years ago a bill was introduced in the Kansas legislature to cut off funds to districts whose children did not score above the national average on such tests. Fortunately the bill did not pass.

Criterion-referenced tests, instead of comparing one child to another, presumably measure the child's performance against a specified criterion or objective. Thus all children might be able to achieve the criterion and eventually score 100 percent on the tests. The criterion-referenced test, in concept, is much like the kind of test the teacher gives in the classroom on Friday to evaluate learning of specific objectives taught earlier in the week.

Conceivably the external criterion toward which the test is directed could be a number of things. For example, one could have a criterion-referenced test for measuring the skills of a bricklayer without reference to how others do. For example: Can he or she lay bricks? Mix mortar? The higher an individual scored on the test, the closer that individual would be to acquiring a bricklayer's skills, regardless of how many other people had the same skills.

Test makers, however, have shown little inclination to develop tests directed toward such criteria. Establishing a sequence of skills and validating them is a laborious, difficult, multiyear task at best. Staying with the example of the bricklayer, they would have to conduct studies to show that good bricklayers score high on the test; that is, they would have to evaluate the test. Test makers instead have resorted to a conception of criterion-referenced tests as those which yield measurements "directly interpretable in terms of specified performance standards."[3] In practice, this means that the criterion toward which the test is directed is usually a prespecified objective or objective stated in advance, e.g., "A bricklayer must be able to mix mortar."

Thus criterion-referenced usually means in practice objective-referenced. In fact, those who have most strongly propagated criterion-referenced testing are frequently the same persons who have propagated behavioral objectives. In typical procedure, objectives are established and test items are written to measure those objectives. Test results can be reported in terms of what specific objectives each individual student was able to achieve, which presumably is useful for instructional purposes. In this way, it is argued, tests can be tailored to specific objectives the way a teacher tailors test questions on what he or she has taught.

The distinction between criterion-referenced and norm-referenced tests is quite blurred. Most test makers use similar procedures to construct items for both types, or use the same item, and employ test statistics for norm-referenced items in selecting items for criterion-referenced tests. There are no clearly defined and commonly agreed upon procedures for constructing criterion-referenced tests, and many of them are in fact norm-referenced tests in disguise. The distinction becomes a matter of emphasis rather than being clear-cut.

Frank B. Womer defines a criterion-referenced test as—

> ...one which is designed to provide information about attainment of a specific objective (criterion), which emphasizes direct measurement through the use of differing formats, which may use items at varying difficulty levels, which must have content validity, which must minimize guessing, and which is particularly useful for instructional and evaluative purposes.[12]

Womer's "differing formats" term indicates he is keen on test items which call for responses other than multiple-choice. Many criterion-referenced tests continue to be made up mainly of multiple-choice items.

A main advantage claimed for criterion-referenced tests is their utility for improving educational programs. In view of the confusion among test makers themselves about the concept, construction, and utility of the tests, some caveats are in order for those considering the use of criterion-referenced or objective-referenced tests:

1. *Common deficiencies in testing need to be communicated both to the profession and to the public. Neither criterion-referenced tests (CRT's) nor objective-referenced tests (ORT's) eliminate the most common deficiencies of tests in general.*

CRT's and ORT's for the most part still measure simple tasks at the expense of relearning abilities and higher-level thought processes.[10] Complex performances are so difficult to measure that test items reflect only the simpler tasks. Such things as Binet's categories of mental imagery, imagination, aesthetic appreciation, and moral sensibility are almost totally unmeasured.

2. *Teachers should examine carefully the derivation of the objectives for ORT's.*

ORT's can be no better than the objectives on which they are based. Unfortunately, the methods for deriving objectives are often ill-considered, hasty, and grossly inadequate. There is an inclination among test makers to slide over the problems of deriving objectives in order to get to item construction, a task with which they are more familiar. Yet appropriate objectives are just as important and just as difficult to arrive at as are test items.

There are at least four ways to choose objectives.[7] First, choosing by *expert judgment* means that a small group of subject matter experts decides which objectives should be measured for a given field. This was essentially the origin of National Assessment tests. While few persons would deny the relevance of the judgments of subject matter experts, few would contend that such judgments faithfully or completely represent what should be taught. By no means do they fully represent the judgments of teachers, parents, students, and others vitally concerned.

A second way of choosing objectives is by *consensus judgment* which requires that various groups—teachers, administrators, parents, school board, etc.—decide what objectives are most important. (For the purposes of this chapter, "objectives" refers to specific student learning outcomes.) Unfortunately, the immense problems of such prioritizing have been slighted. Frequently decision-making groups respond only to those objectives that are presented to them by a single group (e.g., school administrators) or a limited number of groups. Correcting important objectives that have been omitted is not taken into account. If critical objectives do not emerge from the objective-generating process they are ordinarily lost forever. For example, there is likely to emerge a high preponderance of content-bound objectives that are easily measurable. More subtle learnings are neglected. Attending to the objectives that are easily identifiable severely limits the range of decision-makers' thinking and results in determining and limiting the curriculum.

The rating of priority statements themselves is severely dependent upon how abstractly the objectives are specified (i.e., how global they are), the types of criteria on which the objectives are rated (i.e., rated in importance: how much money will be spent on them, how much time and effort will be spent, and the nature of the groups doing the rating).[5,11] Test makers have had little experience polling the opinions of nonprofessional groups, so surveys for the purpose of developing or rating the importance of objectives are likely to be highly class-biased. Actually, such surveys are seldom done. Objectives generation and measurement are likely to be treated in the most cavalier fashion. Test-developers who would never think of including an item without field testing it sometimes accept and discard objectives with abandon. A common procedure is to have the objectives reviewed by a small group of citizens and educators and claim that the objectives have been approved by the public. Those citizens involved are too frequently upper middle-class and the educators are selected in such a way that they are not broadly representative.

A third way of deriving objectives is through *curriculum analysis*. One can inspect materials such as textbooks or courses of study to determine what is being taught and then write objectives and test items based on such content. Much of the impetus for CRT's came from curriculum developers like those who pioneered Individually Prescripted Instruction (IPI) as part of their efforts to develop tests that measure exactly what the materials teach. This procedure also has its limitations in that it is likely to emphasize only content-related objectives.

Fourth, objectives can be chosen by *in-depth analysis of those instructional areas* which one wishes to test. One tries to determine the contents and behaviors in an area of instruction and to associate objectives and test items with contents and behaviors. In other words, by task analysis the instruction is broken into discrete learnings. The most ambitious efforts along this line have resulted in instruments called "domain-referenced tests."[1, 4, 8] Domain-referenced testing (DRT) attempts to define domains of behavior—categories of behavior one might test and teach for—and to represent these domains by an extensive pool of test items which measure human performance in a particular domain or domains. In one sense, domain-referenced tests appear to be an attempt to escape the triviality and absurdity of much of the behavioral objectives movement. If one must delineate a highly specific objective for each aspect of student behavior, one might generate thousands of such objectives. In one project an attempt to define a complete set of objectives for the high school was given up after 20,000 objectives had been written. A complete delineation becomes an absurdity and most such lists become trivial.

Domain-referenced testing aims at overcoming these problems by defining important categories of content and behavior so that only objectives representing particular domains become important. Other objectives are merely subsets or examples. The instructional benefits of such a scheme promise to be large since one could practice on other objectives and test items from the domain to learn the behavior. One could always construct another test from the innumerable objectives and test items representing that domain.

DRT's exist more in promise than in practice. No doubt the task analysts will confront the same formidable conceptual problems as have psychologists who try to categorize mental behavior and curriculum developers who try to define the structure of their subject. Even the most sophisticated schemes of human mental abilities, such as Bloom's Taxonomy, tend to falter when subjected to empirical examination. Human mental processes defy categorization which suggests emphasis on the long-debated principle of teaching to the whole child rather than to specific skills.

3. *Teachers should have an extensive role, from the beginning, in deriving objectives and should beware of co-optation.*

Most teacher and public involvement in developing objectives has been cursory at best—more for the purpose of legitimizing the objectives than for determining or implementing them. For example, objective-referenced tests were developed for the state assessment program in Michigan and employed on a mandatory basis at selected grade levels. For the selected grades, subject specialists from the state education agency set up a small committee developed goals which were later reviewed by subject-matter associations. Then several one-day large group meetings were held around the state to give people a chance to respond.

Despite this effort to involve them, many of the teachers and administrators who participated in the group meetings felt that they had not had adequate input on the objectives.[6] They were presented with a list of objectives and asked to respond after a cursory review. Most teachers in the state never saw or heard of the objectives. In spite of promises that the objectives were only for experimental purposes, the state agency developed tests based on them and administered them the following year, claiming educator endorsement.

4. *Which objectives are selected and retained for testing is critical for ORT's. Teachers should be intimately involved from the beginning in selecting objectives.*

Selection of final objectives for testing is as important as generating them, and teachers are frequently provided only cursory participation in this activity also. In the Michigan assessment program over four hundred objectives were generated for fourth-grade mathematics, yet only thirty-five were selected for testing. The limiting factor was the amount of time required for testing each objective, for it was deemed advisable not to exceed five hours of testing time. Which objectives were excluded? Why? If only the most important objectives were included, how was their importance determined? What would be the instructional effect over time of excluding the other several hundred objectives? In most cases of objective development, the objectives are rewritten and screened by state education agency officials, select citizens' groups, and test makers. For example, in Illinois goals derived from public hearings were selected and extensively rewritten by several groups before being presented as public goals.

5. *The ways in which test items are constructed should be examined. When possible, teachers should employ their own test experts to help them assess the procedures.*

The usual number of items to measure one objective seems to vary from three to five. Good results have been obtained with five. Since even the most specific objective can be measured by thousands of test items, selection is important. Sophisticated test makers use a systematic sampling plan that produces items for subcategories of the objectives.

Of at least equal importance is the type of response the item calls for. Traditional tests use multiple-choice answers because they are easy to score by machine. However, if the purpose of the test is to describe and diagnose classroom learning and provide usable information to the teacher, multiple-choice answers may be much less desirable. The degree to which a test is a faithful sample of learning behavior is more important in an objective-referenced test than in one which merely strives to differentiate among students.

A group of items constructed by teachers is likely to be more relevant to the instruction of those particular teachers. Items written by measurement experts from a matrix of content and behavior are likely to be technically better but less relevant.

6. *CRT's and ORT's should be thoroughly field tested. Teachers should refuse to use tests that have not been thoroughly field tested.*

While this may seem a rather obvious caveat, the fact is that many objective-referenced tests have not been extensively tried out. Even where tried out, frequently only a handful of students are involved. Tests with so little field testing should be resolutely avoided. The test developer should be required to present details of the field test—the test developer who can't probably hasn't conducted one, which is an all too common occurrence.

7. *Test developers should present evidence of the test's reliability. Teachers should not use tests for which evidence on reliability is unavailable.*

For an ORT, each set of items used to measure an objective might be considered a test in itself. These should be reliable measures in and of themselves. The usual reliable determinants are test statistics which are measures of internal consistency developed for traditional norm-referenced tests. They are based on variations in individual test scores—item difficulty and the differences between the top scorers as opposed to bottom scorers, for example. The reliability will be highest when about half of the students get an item right and half get it wrong—a norm-referenced concept maximizing discrimination among test takers.

Using these traditional techniques causes the tests to discriminate in the same way as do items in standardized tests. Unfortunately, the ORT developers have not been able to solve this problem. The alternative is to have no evidence of reliability, which to many is even more unacceptable. Perhaps the best policy is to insist on some measures of reliability, ones for which the test developers supply a public rationale which can be assessed.

8. *The test makers should present evidence of the validity of the tests. Teachers should inspect the validation procedures carefully.*

Validity—which depends upon the ability to answer the question, "Does the test measure what it is supposed to?"—presents another difficult problem for the maker of criterion-referenced tests. For traditional norm-referenced tests, validity is often established by how well the test predicts concurrent academic grades. But this makes little sense for CRT's. Test developers are usually left trying to make logical assessments of content validity based on how the tests were developed.

If the test is objective-referenced, one can assess whether test items adequately measure the objectives and whether the objectives themselves are valid for what the test is trying to measure.

If the test purports to measure the effects of classroom instruction, then the objectives must be the ones taught and the test items must be sensitive to instruction. The Michigan assessment program tried a sensitivity index to determine if correctly responding to an item was dependent on instruction. The index didn't work in this situation. A highly specific objective might be valid for one class but not for another, and a test which presumes to be valid for assessing instruction in a whole state has the problem of demonstrating that its items and objectives were constructed in such a way as to be appropriate statewide—not an easy task. The whole problem of validity is an unresolved one, but the burden of proof should fall on the test maker, not the buyer.

No matter what the derivation of the test or what it is called, unless it covers what a particular teacher has taught it cannot be a valid measure for that teaching situation; it is a measure of someone else's objectives. On the other hand, if the test is a measure of objectives which the teacher developed but which he or she is willing to accept as indicative

of his or her instruction, then the objectives are valid for that teaching situation.

9. *"Minimal competency" or "mastery" cut-off points for students should be viewed with some suspicion. Teachers should question arbitrary standards and substitute their own.*

Item difficulty on tests can be manipulated easily by test makers. Whether a student scores 30 percent or 88 percent can be built into the test itself and just as easily changed by assigning arbitrary values to test items. Since there is no objective means by which tests can establish a level of satisfactory competency, the setting of such standards is extremely arbitrary. What is minimal competency in reading? When has one mastered reading? On the other hand, one may be willing to accept the opinions of certain groups as standards if they are clearly recognized as group opinion and subject to all the deficiencies that implies.

Nonetheless, many CRT developers continue to build highly arbitrary standards into their tests. For example, the Michigan assessment is based on a minimal skill concept that declares a student must achieve 75 percent of the minimal objectives. In the first year of implementation some of the districts where the highest academic achievement might be expected were able to achieve only 30 percent of some objectives. The 75 percent cut-off was evidently without justification.

10. *Many objective-referenced tests are really norm-referenced tests in disguise. No teacher should voluntarily administer a test that he or she does not understand.*

If one constructs objectives such as "reading a newspaper at a fourth-grade level," the norm is obviously built in. If one then selects test items using traditional test statistics, like item difficulty, and uses items from norm-referenced tests, the result is a test that discriminates among students but has the appearance of being referenced to skills rather than students. It becomes a norm-referenced test that looks like a criterion-referenced test. (Some test experts claim that it is impossible to construct anything other than a norm-referenced test.) It is also possible to use ORT results in a norm-referenced manner if one counts how many objectives each student learned and then makes comparisons among students.

11. *The public and the profession should be made aware that CR or ORT's are not panaceas. Test bias problems remain the same with CR or ORT's as with norm-referenced tests.*

Lower socio-economic groups will score as poorly on criterion or objective-referenced tests as they do on norm-referenced tests. Basic factors such as malnutrition and lack of motivation toward school and test taking are untouched by change from one type to another. What CRT's might offer some students is a reprieve from being told they are inferior. (In some districts test scores are attached to the report cards or even reported in the newspapers.) Since self-confidence seems to be critical in schooling, lack of stigmatization could be an important advantage. Another advantage might be to spell out in greater detail where certain educational weaknesses of students lie. Actually, CRT developers have done little that might result in preventing racial, social class, school-building, or neighborhood bias in their tests.

12. *CRT's could cost more than traditional tests, depending on the thoroughness of development. The costs of tests versus their utility should be carefully considered.*

Traditional norm-referenced tests already exist and do not need to be developed, so if CRT superiority can't be positively demonstrated, the question should be raised, "Why go to the extra time and expense?" Also, because of their greater specificity, consider that CRT's might be valid for only a small domain of behavior at a given point in time (there could be large rewards in this, of course, in promoting learning). Many more tests would have to be developed rather than a few general ones. The procedure of developing and validating objectives and test items is a long, difficult, and costly procedure when properly done.

There are two ways of reducing costs. One is based on the assumption that there are certain basic and necessary skills and stages of learning independent of the local setting and that one need develop only one test for basic reading skills and sell it to everyone. This is the assumption of the test makers, but it is a questionable one. Learning

often seems to be highly context-dependent. Children learn in different ways in different settings. The inability of educational research to come up with guaranteed teaching techniques and the inability of psychology to demonstrate transfer of training indicates this is so.

Another way of reducing costs would be to have local groups of teachers develop their own CRT's as they now do for their classrooms. But there is the question of whether the amount of time required would be profitably spent in test construction.[2]

13. *Teachers should not be evaluated on CRT's and ORT's any more than on norm-referenced tests. Teachers should not allow themselves to be evaluated on the basis of ANY tests.*

Tests are not good measures of what is taught in school. Although objective-referenced texts purport to be better measures of learning, they cannot be considered good measures of teaching. An obvious deficiency is that the tests measure only cognitive aspects of the classroom. In addition, the teacher does not have control over many of the variables that affect test scores. Evaluating teachers is a use that should not be claimed for ORT's. The evaluation of teaching should be based on observation, self-evaluation, student ratings, interviews, and many other types of data.

14. *A main advantage of CRT's or ORT's seems to be in the reporting of results, that is, avoiding blanket categorizations of children by test scores and providing more useful instructional information. Subtests should be used only as diagnostic instruments.*

Instead of a composite score with which the teacher can do little but type the child, in criterion or objective-referenced testing the teacher is presented with specific objectives the student can or cannot accomplish. The avoidance of a single score categorizing the child is a major benefit. Presumably the teacher also will be better able to make use of the detailed objectives for improving instruction and learning.

It should be noted, however, that there is little evidence that a teacher can do a better job working with specific objectives than working without them. Whether to use specific objectives should remain a matter of style and judgment for the individual teacher. Robert E. Stake has indicated that there are significant costs in using behavioral objectives, including the possibility that the teacher will teach only what is easy to measure.[10] In Michigan, most teachers did not find the ORT'S valuable for instructional purposes.[6] The instructional benefits are also reduced by the limited number of objectives to which one can teach and for which one can reasonably test.

15. *While worthy of consideration, the claims of criterion, objectives, and domain-referenced tests should be viewed with some skepticism but with an open mind. Teachers should vigorously resist the misuse of all kinds of tests.*

In some ways CRT's can be viewed as a response by the testing establishment to avoid some of the criticisms of tests. Such was the motivation in Michigan. CRT's and ORT's still embody most of the deficiencies of tests in general and are not useful for evaluating teachers in accountability schemes. The tests are also difficult to construct and are subject to much conceptual confusion, even though they do offer the potential of being more useful for instruction.

An important benefit of CR versus norm-referenced tests is that with CRT's the test taker is not stigmatized by a global score supposedly representing his or her ability. This is a great advantage. The best use of tests is in raising questions in the teacher's mind about individual students who achieve unusual scores. The tests themselves may be in error, or the teacher's preconception may be. In any case, following up on seeming discrepancies is the job of the professional. Tests should be used to raise questions, not to resolve them.

GLOSSARY OF MEASUREMENT TERMS*

Achievement Test

A test that measures the amount learned by a student, usually in academic subject matter or basic skills.

Aptitude Test

A test consisting of items selected and standardized so that the test yields a score that can be used in predicting a person's future performance on tasks not evidently similar to those in the test. Aptitude tests may or may not differ in content from achievement tests, but they do differ in purpose. Aptitude tests consist of items that predict future learning of performance; achievement tests consist of items that sample the adequacy of past learning.

Criterion

A standard or judgment used as a basis for quantitative and qualitative comparison; that variable to which a test is compared to constitute a measure of the test's validity. For example, grade-point average attainment of curricular objectives are often used as criteria for judging the validity of an academic aptitude test.

Criterion-Referenced Test

A test in which every item is directly identified with an explicitly stated educational behavioral objective. The test is designed to determine which of these objectives have been mastered by the examinee.

Grade Norm

The average test score obtained by students classified at a given grade placement.

Local Norms

Norms that have been obtained from data collected in a limited locale, such as a school system, county

*Excerpts from the revised edition of *A Glossary of Measurement Terms: A Basic Vocabulary for Evaluation and Testing,* published by CTB/ McGraw-Hill, Del Monte Research Park, Monterey, California 93940. Copyright © 1973. Reprinted by permission of the publisher.

or state. They may be used instead of national norms to evaluate student performance.

Multiple-Choice Item

A test question consisting of a stem in the form of a direct question or incomplete statement and two or more answers, called alternatives or response choices. The examinee's task is to choose from among the alternatives provided the best answer to the question posed in the stem.

Nonverbal Test

A test in which the items consist of symbols, figures, numbers, or pictures, but not words.

Performance Test

A test that requires the use and manipulation of physical objects and the application of physical and manual skills. Shorthand or typing tests, in which the response called for is similar to the behavior about which information is desired, exemplify work-sample tests, which are a type of performance test.

Random Sample

A sample drawn in such a way that every member of the population has an equal chance of being included, thus eliminating selection bias. A random sample is "representative" of its total population.

Reliability

The consistency of test scores obtained by the same individuals on different occasions or with different sets of equivalent items; accuracy of scores. Several types of reliability coefficients should be distinguished.

Coefficient of internal consistency is a measure based on internal analysis of data obtained on a single trial of a test (Kuder-Richardson formulas and the split-half method using the Spearman-Brown formula).

Coefficient of equivalence or alternate forms reliability refers to a correlation between scores from two forms of a test given at approximately the same time.

Coefficient of stability or test-retest reliability refers to a correlation between test and retest with some period of time intervening. The test-retest situation may be with two forms of the same test.

Standardized Test

A test constructed of items that are appropriate in difficulty and discriminating power for the intended examinees and that fit the preplanned table of content specification. The test is administered in accordance with explicit directions for uniform administration and is used with a manual that contains reliable norms for the defined reference groups.

Validity

The ability of a test to measure what it purports to measure. Many methods are used to establish validity, depending on the test's purpose.

THE TESTING OF MINORITY CHILDREN—A NEO-PIAGETIAN APPROACH
by Edward A. De Avila
Barbara Havassy

The National Education Association, the popular press, the courts, civil rights organizations, state and federal agencies, and others have pointed to the failure of the test-publishing industry to consider fully the cultural and linguistic differences of minority children when constructing psychological tests. Test publishers have responded by translating existing intelligence and nationally normed achievement tests into other languages such as Spanish, adjusting norms for ethnic subgroups, and attempting to construct culture-free tests. Each approach involves distinct problems. Moreover, in our opinion, the tests as they are currently designed are of little use to anybody.

Translating existing intelligence or achievement tests for non-English-speaking children often creates problems. First, regional differences within a language make it difficult to use a single translation in a standardized testing situation where examiner and examinee are permitted virtually no interaction. Thus, while *toston* means a quarter or a half dollar to a Chicano, it means a portion of banana squashed and fried to a Puerto Rican.

Second, monolingual translations are inappropriate because the language familiar to non-English-speaking children is often a combination of two languages as in the case of Tex-Mex. Third, many non-English-speaking children have never learned to read in their spoken language. For example, many Chicano children speak Spanish but have had no instruction in reading Spanish.

Another major response of the testing industry to criticism has been to establish or to propose establishment of regional and ethnic norms. Such a practice leads to lower expectations for minorities, which in turn may lower children's aspirations to succeed. Furthermore, ethnic norms do not take into consideration the complex reasons *why* minority children on the average score lower than Anglo American children on IQ tests. Ethnic norms are potentially dangerous from the social perspective because they provide a basis for invidious comparisons between racial groups. The tendency is to assume that lower scores are indicative of lower potential, thereby contributing to the self-fulfilling prophecy of lower expectations for minority chidren and reinforcing the genetic-inferiority argument advanced by Arthur Jensen and others.

In addition, if test publishers and users are willing to establish ethnic norms, they should also establish norms based on sex differences. To take into account both sex and all the ethnic subgroups in the United States would require an almost infinite set of norm tables. From the practical point alone, this is absurd. One might wonder what norms a publisher would use for a set of male/female twins who had a Mexican father and a Hungarian mother.

The testing industry has also responded to criticism of conventional IQ tests by attempting to create culture-free tests. Such tests are difficult to construct, and many question whether they achieve their goal of being free of cultural bias. Tests of mental ability and/or achievement attempt to determine the ability of a child to manipulate certain elements of a problem into a predetermined solution. It is difficult to conceive of test elements equally familiar to children of all ethnic or cultural groups, especially when test developers are members of a group themselves.

In a large number of frequently used IQ and achievement tests, cultural influences on items cause the tests to measure something other than that for which they were designed. Thus, aside from what many tests set out to measure, to a large extent they also measure—

Socialization, Certain test items are actually measures of the child's family value system. In tests marketed in the United States, the referent value system is, generally, that of the Anglo American middle class.

This characteristic is particularly evident in the comprehension scale of one of the major individually administered IQ tests. The test presents questions very much like this one provided by the publisher as a typical, but not authentic, item from the test: "What should you do if you see someone forget his book when he leaves his seat in a restaurant?" This type of question has little or nothing to do with a child's ability to process, manipulate, and/or code information. The answers depend almost exclusively on whether a child has been socialized under the particular ethical system implied by the question.

Productivity cr level of aspiration. Many tests confuse what they hope to measure with a measure of productivity or level of aspiration. For example, in a large number of tests, the child who produces the most responses receives a higher score than the one who stops responding after only a few attempts. The assumption underlying this type of test is that all subjects will produce as many responses as they are able, in other words, that they all have the same level of aspiration.

Timed tests also confuse the measurement of aspiration. In timed tests, which constitute the majority of published group tests, the tester asks children to work quickly, quietly, and efficiently. Little regard is given to children who are not motivated to work in that manner. For the purpose of boosting statistical reliability, tests are constructed in such a way that children are asked a large number of questions which vary only a little in content.

A similar problem involves tests which sequence items in order of increasing difficulty. In these, children encounter increasing levels of failure and frustration. For those who start out fearfully, as do most children unfamiliar with the social demands of the school or test situation, the first indication of failure or difficulty discourages them from continuing.

Experience or specific learning. Tests that require answers of fact assume that all children taking the test will have had about the same exposure to the facts being tested. Any number of examples involving vocabulary bear out the spuriousness of this assumption. It is impossible to determine whether minority children miss a test item because they have never been exposed to the word or because they lack the capacity to understand the word. Problems of this type are found in virtually any test of mental ability which uses

a score on a vocabulary subtest to infer ultimate capability.

One of the most widely used individually administered intelligence tests is full of examples of the importance of specific experience on test results. For example, the child is asked questions of vocabulary which bear directly on past experience or exposure to the words being tested.

Now let us consider the validity and utility of the IQ score. Forgetting for a moment standardized achievement tests, the original justification for the use of the IQ test was that the scores statistically predict mental retardation and low school achievement. Yet in 1971, sociologist Jane Mercer found that of adults who scored below 79 on an individully administered IQ test (and who would have been labeled mentally retarded had they been schoolchildren), 84 percent had completed eight grades or more in school, 83 percent had held a job, 80 percent were financially independent, and almost 100 percent could do their own shopping and travel alone. In other words, even at the task for which experts agree the IQ test is best suited—screening for mental retardation—the IQ measure probably has a dubious real-life validity.

In addition to its traditional use as an indicator of mental retardation, many educators and politicians have come to consider the IQ test to be a useful instrument for teachers, school districts, and state and federal agencies. Indeed, many states mandate that districts administer IQ tests several times as a child goes through the school system. But do the results really help the teacher do a better job?

Let us consider a typical example. A teacher suspects that a child has a severe learning disability and asks the school psychologist to test the child. After the psychologist gives an individually administered test in which the child scores an IQ of 87, the psychologist writes up an extensive report of impressions of the child's performance and potential. Upon receiving the report, the teacher responds in surprise, "But I knew all that. I want to know how I can reach this child." Thus, neither psychologist nor teacher is any wiser despite considerable time and expense administering and evaluating the IQ test.

While few psychologists would agree that educational decisions affecting a child's life should be made just on the basis of an IQ score, the fact remains that such decisions are made by educators who, through personal fiat, supported by state mandate, ignore both individual subscale profiles and psychologists' admonitions for the sake of practical expediency. The result is, of course, a form of default institutional racism.

Thus, while much of the controversy surrounding IQ tests and minority children focuses on whether the IQ model is a valid one, a more practical question concerns the general utility of the information the test produces. In order to answer, one must consider who is asking the question and why. Within the educational system, there are qualitative differences in the type of information needed, depending on the source of the need. To a large extent, much of the confusion surrounding the issue of whether to test stems from failure to consider these differences.

Several levels within the educational system require information traditionally obtained through IQ testing: the funding level which involves federal and state agencies; the local level, which involves district personnel and school principals; and the school level, which involves classroom teacher, para-professional, and parents.

Federal and state funding agencies expect IQ tests to supply them with information concerning statewide or districtwide needs for the purpose of allocating funds and information concerning program effectiveness. There would seem to be far better ways of meeting the first need than trying to infer specific needs from an omnibus assessment based on so poorly understood a concept as IQ. Assessment procedures which can evaluate whether specific educational programs are needed in specific areas such as science would be more useful. Such procedures exist, and these allow direct inference from test performance to program need.

The second need—that of knowing about the effectiveness of particular programs—has become particularly demanding recently in light of accountability and evaluation/audit requirements. In response, these federal and state agencies have often mandated that IQ and standardized achievement tests be administered to evaluate programs.

Actually, program evaluations can be made through a variety of procedures, none of which necessarily has anything to do with IQ or standardized achievement tests. For example, a reasonable assessment can be made by interviewing administrators, teachers, parents, and children as to their perceptions of program effectiveness and by testing specific program objectives and reporting changes in group scores without reference to individual scores.

Local school district personnel require information about the needs of children and the effectiveness of programs in the same way as do the federal and state agencies. However, since needs assessments are usually conducted at the state levels, local officers tend to rely on the state-provided information rather than to conduct expensive research on their own.

Ideally, evaluation of individual programs should center around collection of data dealing directly with program objectives and activities. However, instruments of evaluation often have little to do with the actual program; IQ or nationally normed achievement tests are used, providing scores which often have little in the way of information about effectiveness of individual programs and program components.

The last to be considered in the educational hierarchy are, unfortunately, classroom teachers and what they need to assist the learner. How can teachers translate numerical IQ scores into curriculum or instructional prescriptions? This question is particularly perplexing because teachers cannot rely on absolute point differences on IQ scores. For example, if a teacher wanted to know what should be done differently for children with scores of 92 and 100, the answer would have to be "nothing" because these scores are functionally equivalent. They are both within the "normal" range, i.e., within one standard deviation of the mean. However, when the same eight-point difference is between IQ scores of 84 and 92, there is a different implication. The score of 84 is approximately one standard deviation below the mean and is, in some states, considered to indicate that a child is in the "retarded" or "slow learner" category. In this case, the eight points which separate the 84 and 92 scores would necessitate different recommendations for the children involved.

In many cases, the same criticisms apply to achievement tests that provide collapsed or summary achievement scores. What educational distinctions and decisions can teachers make about children with reading grade equivalency scores of 3.2 versus 3.6 and 3.6 versus 4.0? Neither the IQ score nor the collapsed achievement score provides enough information on which to base sound daily educational decisions.

These issues have brought us to consider an alternative assessment model which derives from the work of Jean Piaget. We have been working with Juan Pascual-Leone of York University, Toronto, in developing a neo-Piagetian procedure, which has been tested with approximately 1,100 Mexican American and other children in four Southwestern states. Children were tested using standardized tests of school achievement, IQ, and four Piaget-derived measures developed individually and jointly by De Avila and Pascaul-Leone over the past 10 years.

The goals of this research were:

1. To test interrelations among the four neo-Piagetian measures in a sample of primarily Mexican American children who live in different areas and have different socioeconomic backgrounds.
2. To examine the psychometric properties of these neo-Piagetian measures.
3. To examine the relation between developmental level as assessed by the neo-Piagetian procedures and IQ as assessed by standardized measures.
4. To examine sex differences in performances on the tests.

Results of this research have shown that:

1. These measures exhibit a developmental progression of performance scores across age in accordance with Piaget's theory of cognitive development.
2. Performance of the primarily Mexican American sample is developmentally appropriate and within the limits of expected levels of cognitive development for given chronological ages.
3. There are no meaningful differences between the sexes.
4. Scores of children taking the tests in English, Spanish, or bilingually showed no appreciable differences.

5. There were no ethnic group differences on the neo-Piagetian measures of cognitive development at the New Mexico location, the only place where direct ethnic group comparisons could be made. There were, however, consistent ethnic group differences on the IQ measures (Otis-Lennon Mental Ability Test) and on the achievement measure (Comprehensive Tests of Basic Skills) always in favor of Anglo Americans.

These results have several implications. First, as this was a field study, further work is needed with greater control over such variables as language background, ethnicity, and achievement. With such controls, the nature of the relationship between neo-Piagetian measures and traditional measures of capacity and achievement can be assessed with greater precision. Second, results of this study indicate that the relationship between cognitive development and school achievement, especially ot Mexican American children, must be more closely examined. Third, the failure to find a difference between Mexican American and Anglo American children on the neo-Piagetian measures leads us to adopt the position that Mexican American children develop cognitively the same as Anglo American children. It appears, however, that cognitive development in Mexican American children and perhaps others is not in itself a sufficient condition to engender a level of school achievement equivalent to that of middle class children.

Failure of Mexican American children to achieve in school and to perform well on traditional capacity and achievement measures must be attributed to reasons other than alleged cognitive inferiority. Some reasons for poor performance, we feel, lie in the design characteristics of curriculum and other classroom materials, language usage, and the situational contexts or givens used in both testing and presenting curriculum. Culturally biased in favor of particular groups, they put all other children at a distinct disadvantage.

While these findings are of importance in understanding the cognitive development of Mexican American children, the more basic question remains: How can the classroom teacher use the information provided by the neo-Piagetian approach on a regular day-by-day basis?

In an attempt to generate test information which directly fulfills informational/instructional needs within the schools, we have designed a computerized system which deals with information needs of the three levels of school personnel discussed previously. At the administrative level, this system provides group statistical data for program evaluation and needs assessment and, at the teacher level, provides classroom recommendations rather than scores.

This system simultaneously takes into account achievement and developmental scores for both the individual child and the child's referent group. It thus becomes possible to determine all of the possible test outcomes and, thereby, to design individual computerized program prescriptions for each child tested. Workshops are then held with the teachers involved to discuss the implementation of these prescriptions. A copy of these recommendations can also be sent to the home so that parents are aware of what the teacher is trying to accomplish with the child and can, with guidance from the teacher, participate in the child's education.

This system, called Program Assessment Pupil Instruction (PAPI), was tested successfully in the same four states where data were gathered for the above described research.

It should be noted that the PAPI system is designed so that a child's peer or referent group can be designated in numerous ways, such as grade, sex, or program group.

Thus far we have tested the PAPI system by working directly with classroom teachers, by explaining the computer printouts, by listening to suggestions, and by continuously refining our approach.

CRITICISMS OF STANDARDIZED TESTING
by Milton G. Holmen
Richard F. Docter

The case for objective assessment of educational achievement through standardized ability testing is based upon the idea that we ought to try our best to measure accurately what children are able to do. Such information, it is argued, should be of value to everyone genuinely concerned with the continuing development and improvement of educational practice. But despite these wholesome goals, educational and psychological testing has come in for a great deal of criticism, especially during the past 20 years. Comment has included allegations that testing is linked to thought-control efforts; that there is manipulation and undue influence on school curriculums, especially at the secondary level; and that tests promote an unwarranted invasion of privacy. Criticisms have come from civil rights spokespersons; from educators; from the critics of education in America; from sociologists, psychologists, philosophers; from politicians, journalists, and public administrators.

Criticisms of testing were especially bountiful in the years between 1955 and 1965. No single focal point of discontent was identified; criticisms, both major and minor, were hurled at testers in schools, in industry and government, and in clinical and research work. (The best summary of this literature is a selected annotated bibliography[1] prepared for the Commission on Tests of the College Entrance Examination Board. A report[2] prepared for this Commission independently catalogs 10 criticisms of tests. Some of these deal primarily with tests of ability or achievement, but most apply also to personality testing.)

In our book, *Educational and Psychological Testing,* we attempt to examine the testing industry and to offer a format to help evaluate the adequacy of testing systems.[3] But in this chapter we have a more limited concern: our goal is to offer a summary of the major criticisms pertaining to standardized educational testing. Please keep in mind that we are not here offering some kind of indictment of this testing; rather, we hope this identification of criticisms will contribute to the responsible development of this important segment of education.

Tests discriminate against some individuals. It has been strongly argued that some testing programs have consistently failed to take into account differences in cultural background and in unique individual attributes. Such failure unquestionably influences test results and may, therefore, penalize the testees.

A major concern is whether tests developed primarily for use with Caucasian subjects can properly be administered to minority-group members. Many of the latter may have educational and cultural backgrounds markedly different from those of the subjects used in the standardization of any particular test.

Employment-selection tests have especially been denounced by minority-group representatives as too often containing built-in bias which favors the middle-class white person and discriminates against the minority applicant. While respected testing professionals may disagree on the interpretation of specific data purported to prove or disprove this point, they agree that tests lacking in job-related validity have no place in selection-and-placement testing programs.

Tests predict imperfectly. No standardized tests are perfect predictors of future behavior. Even the most enthusiastic proponents of objective assessment techniques would insist that their ability to foretell behavior is highly dependent on such factors as the individual(s) to be tested, the behavior to be predicted, the time over which prediction is to be attempted, and the criterion measures used to establish predictive effectiveness.

But even with all these qualifications, critics of testing have come to the conclusion that many tests are weak and unsatisfactory devices which mislead naive test users and result in harm to those tested. Many critics have just about given up on tests, for they see them as falling far short of the ideal applications envisioned by their creators and their publishers.

The problem of test validation encompasses many issues that go beyond establishment of certain formal psychometric properties which may be present to some extent in any test. The proper use of tests must encompass a variety of responsibilities independent of the attributes of any particular test. We must not only ask whether a test has been shown to possess some kind of validity for a known group of subjects, but also must investigate many other questions bearing on the particular circumstances surrounding the application of the test.

Test scores may be rigidly interpreted. Test scores provide one opportunity to establish a data base of individuals. Anyone interested in labeling people can have a field day with test results. This fact notwithstanding, the properly trained user of tests is supposed to know that test scores are not fixed measures, that they are estimates of human attributes at best, and that they necessarily encompass various kinds of sampling errors.

But test scores are often applied in rigid and arbitrary ways. In schools, this can result in assignment of children to ability groupings based on measures which may be indefensible. The quality of professional practice associated with test usage leaves must to be desired.

Tests may be assumed to measure innate characteristics. Some critics of ability testing have argued that tests provide scores that may be naively interpreted as measures of innate characteristics, such as "intelligence"; many harmful consequences are said to flow from this misconception. It has occasionally been assumed that, if tests were not available, people would not make arbitrary classifications of individuals. Tests are therefore condemned as antihumanistic and as fostering a view of humankind that sees human abilities as fixed or rigidly limited.

Even worse, some critics have reasoned that tests influence individuals to conceive of humans in categorical terms, such as "mentally retarded" or "gifted." They conclude that thinking of this kind is undesirable.

At first glance, this seems to be nothing more than a variation on the practice of making rigid use of test scores. The essential difference, however, as expressed by some critics, is that not only do tests foster the belief that one has fixed "intelligence" based on innate characteristcs, but also that the use made of test scores depends heavily on such a belief.

The kind of school program offered and the energy invested in preparing a youngster for the future may be directly influenced by an educator's belief that tests measure innate intelligence. The egalitarian ethic in America frowns upon labeling based on some arbitrary measurement supposed to reflect innate characteristics.

Test scores may influence teacher expectation regarding student potential. In their classic study, Robert Rosenthal and Lenore Jacobson[4] showed that, when teachers' expectations regarding student potentials were based on fictitious information about the students' abilities, the actual achievement of students reflected these expectations. Those who were expected to achieve less did achieve less, and vice versa.

Critics of ability testing have argued with considerable force that tests of "intelligence" have highly undesirable consequences for student performance because, at least in part, teachers tend to relate to students differentially, according to their supposed intelligence. Students who are singled out as "gifted" or "low ability" are given different assignments, rewards, and teachers, and they are systematically taught what is expected of them.

There seems little argument that teachers' expectations contribute to student performance. It is less clear what factors shape teacher expectations. Test scores may be important in determining differences among students for some teachers; however, we need to know far more about the entire matter of teacher expectancy, for many other variables may in fact help to determine their attitudes.

Tests have a harmful effect on the shaping of cognitive styles. The widespread use of multiple-choice test items, matching items, and other test components with a single correct answer is said by some critics of testing to contribute to undesirable styles of thinking. Some claim that the young student is carefully taught that all problems must have a right or wrong answer, and thus the student is led to think in this manner about all questions.

Tests shape school curriculums and restrict educational change. When teachers know that the evaluation of their students will be based on a particular kind of test of some more or less predictable content, they make extensive efforts to assist their students to perform well on these tests. The proponents of statewide testing programs would probably argue that this is exactly what they have in mind—that teachers ought to be encouraged to cover material which their colleagues consider essential. "What's wrong with this?" they ask.

Critics of testing say that experimentation with new ways of teaching, the introduction of new subject matter, and the whole process of individualizing instruction in terms of the needs and interests of individual students are hamstrung by a slavish adherence to standardized achievement testing. The question seems to come down to finding an acceptable balance between the need to know what has been learned during a given period of time and the encouragement of innovation, change, and experimentation in the classroom.

Tests distort the individual's self-concept and level of aspiration. Of all the criticisms of tests, one of the most penetrating and difficult to dismiss is that young persons may generalize from test results and make conclusions about themselves which are not warranted or intended. For example, consider the teenaged boy who is struggling to establish a more positive and more realistic self-concept. How helpful is it for him to be shown his low test scores which may make him conclude that he is far less capable than his classmates?

How many high school students have received brief and inappropriate counseling recommendations, usually based in part on test results, and have concluded from these recommendations that they are not "college material"? One large school district, for example, regularly presents junior high school students with test result summaries printed on cards that the students take home to their parents. These cards offer a lucid and easily understandable summary of what the various achievement and aptitude scores mean. Although the intent is to make information available to parents, there are obviously risks in terms of shaping the attitudes of students toward themselves.

In our view, the proper handling of test results calls for neither a strategy of silence and secrecy nor for open distribution of data without discussion, clarification, and interpretation of meanings.

Tests select homogeneous educational groups. A common procedure in organizing a school is to assign students to classes on the basis of estimates of learning ability. Very often these estimates are based on ability testing. It is a short step to conclude that tests have determined the organizational style of schools, and it may surely

be argued that tests do indeed contribute to the way in which students are assigned.

Critics of the ability-tract system, as this arrangement is often called, frequently see educational testing as the bad guy. But, were no test data available, an educational administrator dedicated to ability-track grouping could find numerous criteria, such as grades, teachers' ratings of ability, and so forth, for making these assignments.

Concerns about homogeneous grouping in schools have acquired strength with recent research which suggests that this allocation procedure tends to do more harm to the low groups than can be justified. The proponents of heterogeneous assignment to classes argue that children with lower ability need the stimulation and the role models provided by higher-ability students if they are to achieve as much as they possibly can.

Contemporary approaches to school organization stress the importance of providing a program of individual instruction for each child, regardless of the range of competences within a class. Educators are now stressing the positive influences of heterogeneous grouping, with the result that the track system is generally thought to be on the way out. But for the parents of children who are assigned to low groups, the track system is an unpleasant reality based primarily on test results. Hence, since tests are often painted as the villain in the situation, it is assumed that banning tests will eliminate the track system.

However, with regard to a school district set on the perpetuation of homogeneous ability grouping, the problem is not so much one of testing or not testing, but rather one of adherence to a questionable concept of educational organization.

Tests invade privacy. School attendance is mandatory for young children. Once in school, the children are generally required to participate in activities, including testing, which some parents consider to be invasions of privacy.

Certainly few would argue against allowing schools to give tests to determine what a student has learned in some course of study, but should schools be allowed to require students to take intelligence tests? What good is such information to a school? Can data from some tests be used to the disadvantage of students without their knowledge that such information even exists? How can the line be more clearly established between information that a school requires to help reach a legitimate decision and information that it has no business acquiring in the first place? The right to privacy is precious to the citizens of a free society; only when there is compelling justification should tests invading privacy be used.

At the heart of the criticisms about tests and testing programs is one fact that is likely to help perpetuate at least some of the criticism: Tests are often used as tools for the allocation of limited resources or opportunities. Put another way, educational and psychological tests are frequently designed to measure differences among individuals so that one person receives a reward or privilege which another is then denied.

For example, we see this in the assignment of elementary school children to classes for the gifted or in the selection of students for college admission or for advanced professional study. Tests, therefore, are likely to stir strong emotions, for they serve in many different ways as gatekeepers, opening and closing pathways of human opportunity.

Are tests necessarily the kind of gatekeepers we want? This is a question involving individual values, organizational goals, and, increasingly, laws and regulations designed to assure equal access to educational and employment opportunities. One thing is certain: Tests are no longer granted any immunity or magical status, or are they assumed to be good simply because of their objectivity or psychometric purity. The lawmaker as well as the citizen on the street has a skeptical eye on educational and psychological testing.

There have been too many serious lapses of professional judgment, not only by those who are using tests without the proper qualifications, but also by professionals who should know better. And minority groups' intense concern for fair play relative to testing is not going to evaporate; indeed, it will probably be expressed with increasing vehemence.

However, while we may anticipate continued criticism of tests for a variety of reasons, testing programs that measure up to high professional standards and can be shown to make constructive contributions to human assessment may well be regarded as beneficial by most people.

PROBLEMS IN USING PUPIL OUTCOMES FOR TEACHER EVALUATION
by Robert S. Soar
Ruth M. Soar

During the past few years there has been mounting pressure for measuring the outcomes of education, with movement toward holding the teacher, the school, and the school system accountable for producing the student learning expected by society. Decreasing enrollments, tighter budgets, and a general trend toward cost effectiveness have added to the pressure.

Measuring pupil achievement increasingly has been proposed as a way of assessing the effectiveness of teaching and, in fact, has been mandated by a number of states. This approach is superficially reasonable and attractive, but it is fraught with problems which have not been generally recognized.

H. L. Mencken once commented, "There's always a well-known solution to every human problem—neat, plausible and wrong." The use of pupil achievement as a way of evaluating the teacher, the school, or the school system embodies this misleading simplicity. The solution seems so straight-forward: If the job of teachers is to promote learning in pupils, then it seems reasonable to evaluate them in terms of the amount of learning they produce in their pupils.

The parallel with the industrial setting is clear: If the job of a worker is to assemble relays, then it seems reasonable to count the number of relays the worker assembles and pay him or her accordingly. But in applying this procedure to teaching, a number of problems emerge that have not been widely recognized. The relay assembler receives parts which are identical (at least within very close limits) on which he or she performs a prescribed set of operations, also identical. Then each completed units leaves the assembler, again almost identical to the others.

But none of this is true for teachers. Pupils appear in the classroom differing in ability, level of achievement, home background, interest, motivation, age—differing in numerous ways. Teachers must recognize these differences as they strive to help individual pupils grow toward their own potentials. Consequently, the teaching process will differ from pupil to pupil. If the teacher has been successful, each pupil will have improved educa-

tionally when he or she leaves the classroom but each will probably be no more like the others than when the year began.

A major dimension, then, of the problem of evaluating teachers in terms of pupil outcomes is the recognition that what goes on in the classroom is not the only, or the most powerful, influence on where a pupil stands in achievement at the end of the year.

Research has shown that the differences pupils bring with them when they enter the classroom have significant influence on achievement. Entry level ability (pretest or fall score) and socio-economic status are major determinants of what a pupil's standing will be at the end of the school year. These influences probably are more widely accepted than any other, but they are highly interrelated so that one overlaps the other. In practice they cannot be effectively separated.

The fact that IQ and achievement scores in the fall are highly related to spring achievement scores is widely accepted but seldom documented. In a study of 81 fifth-grade classes, R. S. Soar and R. M. Soar[16] found correlations between class averages (means) for fall IQ and spring achievement ranging from +.85 to +.90, and correlations between fall achievement and spring achievement ranging from .75 to .85. So the evidence is that as much as 80 percent of the variation in class averages for pupil achievement at the end of the year can be accounted for by pupil characteristics which existed at the beginning of the year, characteristics over which the teacher has no control.

The most extensive data on the influence of socio-economic status on pupil achievement were presented in the Coleman Report, and more recently and more widely re-analyzed by F. Mosteller and D. P. Moynihan[11] and G. W. Mayeske, and others.[9] The studies show that as much as 80 percent of the variation in pupil achievement across schools (equal to a correlation of about +.90) can be accounted for by these factors.

Beyond these major influences there are others which help account for differences in pupil achievement and which should be considered. Although the research on family attitudes and support for learning in the home is not as extensive as that for pupil ability (pretest) and social status, it is consistent in indicating relationships between the educational values held by parents and their children's achievement in school. M. Garber and W. B. Ware[6] found a relation of +.47 between achievement and a combined measure of support for learning in the home for a group of Black and Spanish-American children. All students in the sample met federal poverty guidelines, so that socio-economic status as usually measured was, in effect, held constant. The same authors cite similar findings from other studies.

Peer group attitude, although again the research is not extensive, has been identified as another important factor which can either support or hinder a pupil's achievement.[1]

Since there is compelling evidence that a number of influences over which the teacher has no control have powerful effects on pupil achievement, it cannot be expected that a teacher will have consistent results with successive groups of pupils. That is, the teacher will not be equally effective in producing growth with all groups because groups differ so widely. Studies by Barak Rosenshine[13] and J. E. Brophy,[3] for example, show that on the average only about 10 to 15 percent of the variation in achievement from group to group reflects the stable influence of the teacher, as shown by a median correlation in the low .30's.

As D. M. Medley[10] has pointed out, and as commonly accepted methods[4] of estimating reliability show, data from about twenty classes would be required for making reliable decisions about individual teachers. Given this requirement necessitating collection of such large amounts of data, using the measurement of pupil achievement as a way to evaluate teachers is impractical as well as invalid.

What these findings seem to indicate is that the education of the pupil is dependent on many conditions in the society, not on the school alone. When the time the pupil spends in the classroom is compared with the time spent under other influences, and when the degree of influence or control the teacher can exercise is compared with the power of other influences, the limited effect of the teacher is not surprising.

Because influences other than the teacher make a major difference in how much the child learns is not to say that the role of the teacher is unimportant. The teacher is the only formal, institutionalized input which society makes for the education of the child and the transmission of an established curriculum. And much of what the teacher does that contributes constructively to the child's future abilities, successes, and satisfactions may not be measured by currently common achievement instruments. It does say, however, that the influence of teachers is limited and that teachers are most effective when they have the support of other elements in the society.

This whole constellation of other influences is usually not given consideration when measures of pupil achievement are proposed as the basis for evaluating teachers. It is reasonable that these influences are strong, since they accumulate over the life of the pupil. It is obvious, then, that pupil standing at the end of any school year is a completely inadequate and even misleading measure of the effectiveness of the teacher or the school. Yet the results of such achievement standings are frequently published by school or by school system.

"Achievement," which is the most frequently used measure of student learning outcomes, usually refers to the amount of knowledge a pupil possesses at a given point—his or her "standing." The influences cited above show a strong relation to achievement as used in this sense.

An alternative to measuring achievement standing is to measure change in achievement from the beginning to the end of the year. When this is done, the influences cited are still likely to have an effect, although to a lesser degree, since change reflects their influence for a shorter period of time.

Although this alternative is appealing as another way of evaluating teaching, it raises still other problems. In a classic volume on the problems of measuring change, C. Bereiter[2] commented:

> Although it is commonplace for research to be stymied by some difficulty in experimental methodology, there are really not many instances in the behavioral sciences of promising questions going unresearched because of deficiencies in statistical methodology. Questions dealing with psychological change may well constitute the most important exceptions. It is only in relation to such questions that the writer has ever heard colleagues admit to having abandoned major research objectives solely because the statistical problem seemed to be insurmountable.

If the fall score is simply substracted from the spring score so as to obtain a measure of net change, a new set of subtle but difficult problems is created. An illustration many serve to identify some of them. Firgure 1 presents fictitious data from a group of pupils for whom measures of IQ from two forms of a test have been obtained 10 days apart. The initial IQ's are plotted on the baseline and the second IQ's on the vertical axis. Any point in the area outlined by the ellipse represents simultaneously the IQ of a pupil on each of the testings, and the high and low 10 percent of the pupils at each of the two times has been indicated by shading and cross-hatching.

It is clear that the pupils who were in an extreme group on the first test were not, for the most part, in an extreme group on the second test. The blackened areas represent the small number of pupils who were extreme on both occasions.

At the upper right, the area is small because the pupils who make the highest scores at any testing are likely to do so on two bases: (1) they are bright (have high verbal skills), and (2) they are lucky (that is, they happen to make good guesses on a few items for which they aren't sure of the answer, or the items on this test just happen to be ones for which they know the answers). But they are not likely to be lucky consistently when another form of the test is given, and so on another testing their scores are likely to be lower. Opposite influences will affect pupils at the lower left end of the ellipse.

To put it another way, if the cutting point for the top 10 percent is an IQ of 120, there will be a number of pupils with true IQ's close to 120 who will sometimes be above that score on a series of tests and sometimes below it, depending on chance factors. So some fraction of pupils above 120 on the first test will fall below it on the second. Similarly, some of the pupils scoring below 80 on the first test will be above it on a second.

In both cases, extreme pupils have regressed, or moved, toward the mean. This regression effect can be expected whenever prediction is less than perfect, and the extent of the movement will depend on the inaccuracy of the prediction.[7] With most psychological or educational predictions, the regression involved is considerable and may make up a significant proportion of the total range of scores.

The point to be stressed from this example has important consequences: Since pupils who were in the bottom 10 percent the first time were not, for the most part, in that group the second time, they must have moved upward. Similarly, the pupils in the top group must have moved downward. That is, there is a negative relationship between initial standing and the direction in which change is most likely.

As an example of this effect, the pupils who stand highest on an achievement measure at the beginning of the school year will probably show little if any increase in score at the end of the year, and may even show a decline. On the other hand, pupils who score lowest at the beginning of the year will probably show considerable increase. Educators have sometimes been misled by this effect and have assumed that their programs were more functional for low achieving pupils than for high achieving pupils, when in reality all that was involved was the regression effect (the statistical tendency for scores to move toward the average). Similarly, a group of pupils placed in a remedial program because they stand low on a pretest can be expected to show considerable improvement; but again the improvement may be spurious, as a consequence of the regression effect.

This problem creates real difficulties if pupils are tracked on the basis of fall scores and teachers are evaluated on the basis of change in achievement of their pupils. For example, assume that pupils are tested in reading in the fall and the lowest third are put in Ms. Jones' class, the middle third in Mr. Smith's class, and the highest third in Mrs. Williams' class. We can anticipate that at the end of the year Ms. Jones' class will show much improvement and Mr. Smith's will show modest gain, but Mrs. Williams will be fortunate if her pupils show any growth at all. The problem is that the gain the pupils show is materially affected by regression effect, so to evaluate the teacher on the basis of pupil gain would be manifestly unfair.

There are statistical procedures for attempting to eliminate this effect, but as C. Bereiter[2] commented, it is impossible to be certain that appropriate adjustments have been made; and the expertise to do even the best that can be done with the problem is not widespread. And, of course, all the out-of-school influences on achievement standing discussed earlier also influence gain,

Figure 1

An Illustration of Regression Effect

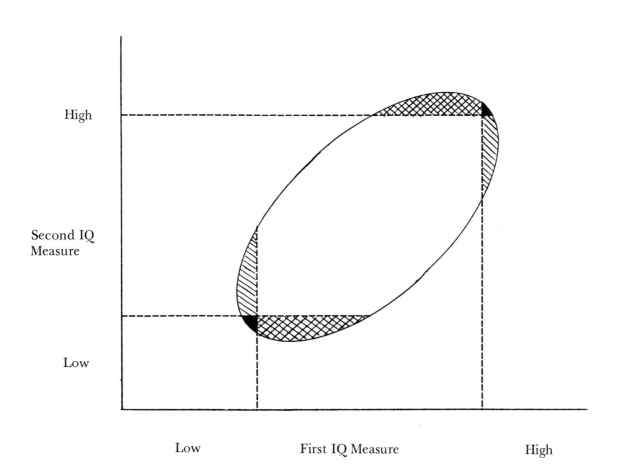

although to a lesser degree. So it is clearly inappropriate to use pupil change as a way of evaluating teachers where a teacher may suffer as a consequence of the error involved.

A procedure for evaluating teachers which attempts to bypass the problems of change is the performance test or the evaluative teaching unit.[5] In it, the teacher teaches a prescribed brief unit (sometimes as little as a few minutes or as much as two weeks) and pupil knowledge is then tested. The attempt is made to minimize the problems of measuring gain by teaching material in which pupils should have little or no preknowledge, so that all presumably start at the same level. But the other problems of using pupil achievement to evaluate teachers still apply. In addition, there are questions of whether teaching material which does not have to be integrated into previous knowledge requires the same skills as the usual teaching setting and whether such short-term learning generalizes to long-term learning. There is the final difficulty that the performance of teachers on a unit of a few minutes does not predict their performance on a two-week unit.[8] Assuming that either can be used to predict year-long performance then seems risky. Even if the measurement of standing or gain in achievement were a satisfactory way of evaluating teachers, there is still the problem of selecting the objectives to be measured.

Although subject matter achievement has been the primary focus of the discussion thus far, it is clear that schools are charged with and have accepted some degree of responsibility for many other kinds of pupil growth. Over a long period schools have given attention to the social development and the moral values of pupils. And a broad view of the relationship between school and society suggests that when a problem emerges in the society, one of the first steps is likely to involve the school in solving the problem. Traffic problems led to driver education; a concern for the loyalty of government employees led first to a ban on teaching about communism in the schools and later to the requirement that it be taught; problems of drug abuse have led to drug abuse education in the schools; concern about sexual attitudes has led to sex education; concern for occupational choice has led to career education in the schools; and when concern for segregation of the races became pressing for the society, the first and the major attempt to deal with the problem was delegated to the schools. To evaluate teachers and schools solely on the basis of the subject matter gains made by pupils grossly underrepresents the broad range of objectives for which teachers and schools have been given some degree of responsibility. Yet for many of these objectives there are no measures which are immediately, for some even remotely, available.

Even within the subject-matter realm there are problems which are largely ignored. One of these problems is the need to distinguish complex achievement growth from simple growth and to provide appropriate measurement for each. Memorization of facts (rote memory) falls at the simplest level and complicated problem-solving, abstracting, and generalizing fall at the most complex level; the difference is between retrieving information (memory) and processing information in its varying degrees of complexity. There is some evidence from a number of studies that the teaching behaviors which are associated with greatest growth in simple tasks are different from those which are associated with greatest growth in complex tasks. [15,16,17,18].

Most studies of pupil achievement fail to make this distinction; and the current stress on criterion-referenced measurement, emphasizing small-step learning, seems likely to focus on simple kinds of learning. Measures of complex learning are slow and difficult to construct, in contrast to measures of simple learning, which can be more easily and quickly developed. Evaluating all subject matter at all grade levels would almost certainly require the construction of many new measures which would likely emphasize simple kinds of achievement, given the ease with which they can be constructed and the emphasis on criterion-referenced measurement. If teachers were to be evaluated on the basis of pupil achievement, then it seems likely that the teacher who emphasizes simple learning would be evaluated more positively than the teacher who emphasizes complex learning. This would be an unfortunate result.

A further problem related to the difficulty of measuring complex achievement growth is the likelihood that some highly valued objectives grow too slowly to show change within a school year—objectives such as complex problem-solving skills, citizenship, attitudes, learning to get along well with others, and creative expression. On the other hand, it seems likely that measures of short-term learning would tend to emphasize simpler kinds of learning.

A description of an application of accountability in England a century ago makes one of the problems clear.[14] In that setting, teachers were evaluated on the number of their pupils who attained the minimum level of achievement expected for the particular grade. The result was that teachers concentrated their efforts at the minimum level of proficiency, with a consequent lowering of the quality of instruction.

Another problem of serious consequence in the use of pupil measures is raised by the OEO study of performance contracting, which found that the superior achievement of performance-contracting programs disappeared when the teaching was controlled to eliminate the possibility of teaching the test.[12] It seems clear that, in a setting in which financial return follows from pupil achievement, teaching the test is likely to occur at least a portion of the time. This is a very reasonable finding and one which is well known, even in cases where a financial return is not involved—teaching to the Regents Examination, for example.

A final problem is the possibility of bias if the teacher is the test administrator. Even outside test administrators have difficulty not helping pupils. Where a teacher is affected personally, it seems

possible that his or her behavior might be influenced, even though unconsciously. This problem could be dealt with by using only specially trained test administrators, but this could be very costly.

When all these problems in the use of pupil achievement for teacher evaluation are considered, they become overwhelming. The influence of the teacher is minor compared to the out-of-the-classroom influences—pupil ability, previous knowledge, the home, the peer group, motivation, and others. What the pupil brings to the classroom in this respect is clearly a much stronger determinant of where he or she will stand at the end of the year than anything that have been done in the classroom. Influences on the development of future achievement measures seem likely to limit them to relatively simple measures for some time to come. Tests available for measuring the other objectives for which the teacher is to some degree responsible are relatively few. In addition to these problems, there are statistical difficulties in the measurement of change which are extremely serious, if not disabling. They are still further exacerbated by the likely problems of teaching the test, of the teacher giving attention primarily to a small portion of the students, and of obtaining valid measurement in the classroom.

Taken all in all, this is an imposing array of difficulties, most of which have gone unrecognized when it is proposed that teachers be evaluated by measuring the outcomes of their pupils.

TEACHER-MADE TESTS—AN ALTERNATIVE TO STANDARDIZED TESTS

by Frances Quinto

Developing tests for classroom use is a routine activity for most teachers. These tests, a form of the criterion-referenced type, serve the needs of both the student and teacher. They disclose where the student stands in relation to classroom objectives and guide the teacher in providing the student with appropriate help. Because of the information that tests can offer, they should be developed carefully rather than "off-the-top-of-the-head."

What are some elements that can make teacher-developed tests effective? How can teachers be certain that a test will reveal the kinds of information they want?

Some teachers and test developers have found the following procedures to be of value:

The teacher should decide the purpose of giving the test and know how the results will be used. A teacher can give a test to determine a group's strengths and weaknesses or to measure a class's or an individual student's knowledge of subject matter. The teacher can give the test upon first meeting a class, before introducing a unit of study, or after completing a unit or course. A test can be a reinforcement activity or an instructional device, or it can be the "every-Friday" test which helps students and instructor to monitor progress in an orderly fashion. It can help the teacher identify the students who need special help and the areas in which they need the help. It can also be a means of observing special talents.

A first step in preparing a test is listing the kinds of information to elicit and then deciding on the best format for getting that information. The format can be essay, problem solving, computational, application of information in new situations, multiple-choice, or a combination of these. The format of a test is determined by the subject area, the kinds of information needed, and the amount of time allotted for the test. The teacher should decide what number or percentage of questions to put in each category.

Multiple-choice questions are difficult to develop, so they take the most time prior to administering the test. Essay questions take less time to develop, but much more time to evaluate.

Just as variety is necessary in classroom activity, so it is necessary in tests. Therefore, teachers will want to include some items that students can work through quickly and others that they will work on for somewhat longer periods of time.

If reading comprehension or other reading abilities are not being tested, then written questions and problems, including directions, should be easy enough for all students to understand, or else teachers should give directions orally.

Generally teachers like the challenge of creating new problems. Good tests are not simple to construct, however. Teachers should save effective items or exercises from year to year. In that case, they should review the items before using them to be sure that all the areas they deal with have been covered in class. Whether test items are newly constructed or taken from a previous test, the person who developed the test or another instructor should take the test to be sure it is fair in presentation and content.

Test items may be confusing or ambiguous; reviewing the corrected tests will help teachers to discover weaknesses.

Teachers should not construct questions to stump, catch, or confuse, but should state them as clearly as possible. In a multiple-choice sequence, the right and wrong answers should not be too close in meaning. A "distractor"— the wrong multiple-choice answer—should not be the correct answer to another question, because this may confuse students. Tests should help students clarify their thinking—not confuse it.

For essay questions, teachers would be wise to devise a key or scoring guide that they can use for both commenting and assessing. They can assign weights to such factors as organization of topic, description, and grammar. They should use the key consistently. Teachers of subjects like science or sociology must be consistent, too, in the weight they give punctuation and grammar in evaluating their tests.

True-false tests, which supposedly measure students' command of facts, are the simplest to construct. They should not be used as a major basis for judgments about progress because chance—and guessing—affect their results. Teachers have argued that some credit should be given for items not answered on true-false tests, since these can give the teacher a truer picture of the group's knowledge.

Here are additional suggestions that can be useful in constructing tests:

- In a true-false test, about one-fourth of the items should be false. Students are afraid to trust their own judgment when too many are false.
- Items should be arranged from easy to hard so that the beginning of the test will give students confidence.
- The first and last items of a test should concern an obvious, mainstream topic so that students will leave the test feeling satisfied.

- Questions should be worded in the positive, and positive and negative questions should not be combined in the same section of the test. After a series of positive questions, students have trouble answering those worded in the negative because the mental shift is tricky.

In an effort to depart from the old-fashioned true-false, multiple-choice exercises, teachers may want to prepare items that stretch the students' imagination. Teachers can prepare exercises that allow students to estimate "how far," "how many," "what kinds of," and the like. Students enjoy and can benefit from exercises which allow them to make inferences, such as "What effects will be felt in the community as a result of (such and such) court case (decision)?"

Creativity in test-making is an art. The artfulness does improve with practice, and the improvement can benefit both student and teacher alike.

AN ALTERNATIVE TO BLANKET STANDARDIZED TESTING
by Richard J. Stiggins

It is common practice among some public school districts to have a committee of teachers and administrators annually review the district testing procedures. The committee usually discusses what standardized achievement test battery and/or aptitude or intelligence tests should be used at what grade levels. And the result is generally a rubber stamp on previously used procedures.

Recently, however, a number of innovations in testing procedures have emerged which may make rubber stamping inappropriate. They include the use of sampling procedures and such innovations as criterion- and domain-referenced testing.

For a number of reasons, however, these innovations are not frequently part of the test review committee's deliberations. One reason may be the committee members' limited knowledge about testing, which is a highly technical subject and does not lend itself easily to simple explanation, understanding, and application.

The institutionalization of testing procedures has also contributed to the lack of knowledge and applications of innovation in educational testing. Or as Samuel Superintendent might put it, "The board of education will never let us give up standardized testing."

A third and final reason for the lack of impact of educational measurement innovation on public education is the minor role that tests play in educational decision making. Because of their general nature, standardized tests are limited in their ability to contribute to district, school, or classroom level decisions. Many educators may recognize this fact and yet continue to give the tests because their use satisfies the board and the public.

In brief, a lack of technical knowledge of testing has given rise to the three factors stated above, each of which in turn prevents the gaining of new knowledge of testing. The result is a closed system of development in educational testing which resists the implementation of practices and procedures common to other fields.

One such practice is sampling, a procedure for increasing the efficiency of data collection that is gaining prominence in educational testing as a result of recent large-scale testing programs, such as the National Assessment of Educational Progress.

Random sampling is a statistical procedure which allows such social scientists as Gallup, Harris, and other pollsters to draw general conclusions about the attitudes of an entire population on the basis of a very few scientifically selected respondents. Survey participants are randomly selected to be representative of larger groups, thus allowing for efficient, less expensive, and quite accurate conclusions.

And so it can be with achievement test scores. In situations where testers want to draw general conclusions about large groups of students, such as an entire grade level for a district, a properly selected sample can yield very accurate estimates of "typical student" performance.

Another innovation in educational testing situations, matrix sampling takes advantage of just such a random sampling procedure to increase efficiency by reducing the number of students involved in testing. But there is another sampling dimension. Not only is it unnecessary for each student to be tested to generate accurate group estimates of academic performance, but it is unnecessary for every student to respond to every test item.

Matrix sampling involves the simultaneous random sampling of both students and test items. It involves, however, different, nonoverlapping samples of students taking nonoverlapping samples of items so that each matrix sample is a sample of students taking a sample of items.

This requires a set of items to be partitioned randomly into several subsets and each subset given to a different sample of students. For example, if there are 50 items, they could be partitioned into 10 samples of 5 items each and each sample randomly assigned to 1 of 10 samples of students.

The procedure reduces the number of students and the amount of class time required to generate the desired data. When responses to items are summarized, the results may be generalized to both the entire test from which the items were derived and the entire population of students from which the sample was selected. It is important to note, however, that no information is gathered on individual pupil performance. A matrix sample provides only group estimates.

Let me illustrate why matrix sampling might be useful and appropriate for an annual district-wide standardized testing program.

I will argue that the only truly legitimate concerns of standardized testing in any district are general conclusions about the entire student body. Testing is one process of gathering information for decision making. In education, decisions have to be made at a number of levels.

First, we must make diagnostic and prescriptive decisions regarding individual students. Second, we must make decisions regarding the viability of specific educational programs. (This is the newly emerging concern for program evaluation.) In addition, building administrators must make general school-level decisions. Finally, superintendents, boards of education, and the public must make district-level decisions.

In most districts, the information on educational outcomes required for many of these multi-level decisions is typically generated from the annual administration of a standardized achievement battery. The computer scoring service is then able to return individual pupil scores, class averages, building averages, and district summaries, all for about 75¢ to $1 per student. This seems most economical until one considers what actually happens to these test scores and summaries.

First of all, at the classroom level, these scores are designed to discriminate among students "to help with diagnosis." However, I challenge anyone to diagnose and prescribe from a grade equivalent of 3.2 in a general gross construct called "total reading." Most teachers recognize that such transformed scores contain too little information to be diagnostic or prescriptive.

The test publishers argue that teachers can do individual item analysis to reveal specific weaknesses, but any teacher who has attempted to do this realizes how tedious this task can be.

At the specific program level of decision making, standardized achievement batteries also fall somewhat short of necessary data requirements. The qualities of items selected to allow the test to discriminate among students make it very difficult for them to detect specific educational program impacts. The items are simply too short, too general, and too individualized to be sensitive to local instructional interventions.

For example, correct responses to four additional test items represent a year's growth in grade equivalent terms between grades five and six on the *Iowa Test of Basic Skills,* Form 5, Level 12, Arithmetic Concepts. Not only is it totally unfair to characterize an individual learner's year of growth so narrowly, but as a program developer, I would be quick to challenge an evaluator who selected such an imprecise tool to demonstrate the viability of my newly developed instructional sequence. From a program evaluation point of view, instruments more sensitive to local program objectives are much more desirable for program decision making than are any national standardized examinations.

Many of the problems which arise from using standardized tests as criteria for judging specific program quality also arise when one attempts to differentiate among general program elements, such as classes, teachers, departments, or buildings. Because of the lack of sensitivity of these tools, there is little or no educational research delineating any causal line between program elements and standardized outcome measures.

To say that one school's learning environment is better than another's or one principal is more competent than another on the basis of standardized test data is a total misuse of the data. Yet the summaries returned to districts by scoring services and comments of educators would suggest that this is the intent.

To date, educational research can establish no significant stable links between any teacher, administrator, or building characteristics and differential standardized achievement test scores. Therefore, it is quite apparent that standardized test scores are incapable of contributing to specific and general program-related decisions.

What, then, are these tests capable of doing? Very simple, they are useful as gross indicators which can best serve as information for communication to the public on the state of achievement in a given district. In fact, it may be that this is the only real use they are put to in most districts anyway.

If these tests are really incapable of contributing to important specific decisions, then their use for public relations is their only appropriate use. In that case, a testing system which yields only the district average data would be sufficient. Such a system can be created by using sampling procedures. An investment of hundreds of dollars for sample data can provide information of the same value as that previously gathered for thousands. The dollar savings can be used to gather other types of outcome data which are prescriptive and appropriate for program-related decisions.

A SUMMARY OF ALTERNATIVES

NEA Resolution on Standardized Tests

76-65. The National Education Association strongly encourages the elimination of group standardized intelligence, aptitude, and achievement tests.

In a final report to the NEA Representative Assembly, the NEA Task Force on Testing recommended that alternatives to group standardized testing be developed. In keeping with that recommendation, the following brief descriptions of alternatives are presented.

Anecdotal Records

Recording the behaviors of individual students reveals more about a student than do test results. A teacher can develop a composite picture of a student by observing and recording behavior such as interaction with others, motivational patterns, and independent work habits.

Teachers who have set about keeping anecdotal records report that not only is the experience satisfying for them, but that they improve with practice and constantly get new insights into a student that either support or explain other evaluation results.

Oral Presentations by Students

Students' oral presentations have long been accepted as one way to evaluate student progress. For example, skilled reading teachers use them both in evaluating student progress and in diagnosing specific difficulties. Subject matter teachers can assess both depth of knowledge and personal capabilities using this mode of performance.

In assigning oral presentations to students, teachers must state clearly beforehand what is expected of the students and what are the criteria for a good performance. The structure offers the opportunity for self- and peer evaluation, particularly when oral presentations are recorded.

Contracts with Students

A contract or agreement between student and instructor specifies tasks that both parties must complete within a given period of time. An instructor carefully poses problems with varying degrees of difficulty, and students, with teacher guidance, select both the problems they will work on and the amount of time they will spend on them. Ability to perform the tasks is measured by promptness and accuracy in completing the contract items. Requiring students to work alone, as contracts generally do, adds to an instructor's understanding of a student's academic and personal development.

Student Self- and Peer Evaluation

Students can be, and ought to be, involved in evaluating their own work. The ability to assess one's performance is useful in ways that transcend school learning. Students can become more insightful about themselves and their approach to work.

Self- and peer assessment is complex, particularly when more than simple student products are being judged. When expressing subjective judgments, students tend to underrate rather than overrate their own abilities and achievements. Because of this, some background and skill on the part of teachers is required in dealing with sensitive affective areas and development of self-concepts. Many well-developed approaches exist for such purposes.

Parent-Teacher Conferences

The purposes of most parent-teacher conferences are for the parties to exchange information about a student that will help to guide him or her into productive channels and to find ways in which he or she can secure satisfaction and growth. These conferences are valuable when there is thoughtful preparation and when they are used as a supplement to written evaluations. They also offer an excellent opportunity to relate schooling to the home—a necessary adjunct for a vast majority of students.

Objectives-Referenced (Criterion-Referenced) Tests

The potential advantage of these tests over standardized tests is that students are judged on their mastery of objectives rather than on their standing in relation to others. In this way, they serve some diagnostic purposes. At this time, these tests have not had wide enough use to confirm fully their value, particularly when broad subject areas must be considered. If the original intention of criterion-referenced tests is not distorted, they have great potential as an alternative to standardized tests.

Individual Diagnostic Tests

These sophisticated evaluation devices are reliable and valid for specific purposes. They are underused because administering them is frequently time-consuming and expensive. Also applying, scoring, and analyzing individual diagnostic tests often requires special training that is generally not available to teachers.

Nevertheless, these tests have the potential of providing additional information the teacher can use in prescribing learning strategies for a student.

Teacher-Made Tests

Good examples of objectives-referenced tests are those constructed by teachers for their own use. These can closely reflect the content and emphasis of classroom subject matter, and teachers can use the results in making decisions that are as diverse as the pace of instruction; prescriptive assignments; reporting to or conferring with parents; and promoting or retaining a student. This broad range of decisions requires that teachers be familiar with methods of constructing classroom tests which will measure both factual knowledge and higher levels of thinking.

School Letter Grades

Conventional grading systems of A, B, C, D, or E or equivalent designations (percentages/averages) are, for the most part, understandable to parents and acceptable to students. Giving grades can be particularly valuable when teachers use descriptions to expand and to clarify the meaning of the grades. Even such limited descriptors as *excellent, satisfactory,* and *needs improvement* may be more useful to parents and students than the standardized test statistic of "10 standard score points above the mean."

Open Admissions

In a strict sense, the policy of open admissions is not an alternative to testing but a practice that indicates change in college requirements. It could eliminate the need for standardized tests.

Many institutions of higher education now accept all students who have completed high school; they give no consideration to scholastic-aptitude or achievement tests. Some universities admit fourth year high school students into their freshman classes upon the recommendation of high school teachers. Adult education and life-long learning programs provide access to degree-granting programs for working people. Combinations and variations of the above offer opportunities which in the past would have been highly unusual if not totally unacceptable.

The criterion for admission to these schools is the desire to be educated rather than the score achieved on a standardized test.

The full story is not yet in on the success of these programs, but the concept of openness provides for more equitable educational opportunities for all. This holds true for other levels of schooling.

TESTS AND USE OF TESTS:
NEA CONFERENCE ON CIVIL AND HUMAN RIGHTS IN EDUCATION, 1972

SOCIOCULTURAL FACTORS IN THE EDUCATION OF BLACK AND CHICANO CHILDREN
by Jane R. Mercer

Studies dating back to the 1930's have demonstrated the cultural biases inherent in IQ tests and other standardized achievement measures. Yet clinicians have continued to interpret children's performances on these tests as if there were no biases and have never systematically taken sociocultural differences into account when interpreting the meaning of a particular child's score. Consequently, we find many children in classes for the mentally retarded whose adaptive behavior in nonacademic settings clearly demonstrates that their problems are school specific and that they are not comprehensively incompetent.

Disproportionately large numbers of Black, Chicano, and probably Puerto Rican children are labeled mentally retarded by the public schools. In California, the rates for placing Chicano and Black children in classes for the mentally retarded are two to four times higher per thousand than for English-speaking Caucasian children, or Anglos.

The public schools label as retarded a large number of children who are not so regarded by their families, neighborhoods, churches, or other community organizations. We asked 241 organizations in a Southern California city for information on each retarded person they were serving. The public schools listed far more retardates than any other formal organization, shared their labels with more other organizations, and labeled as retarded more persons with IQ's above 70 and with no physical disabilities. There were 4½ times as many Chicanos and twice as many Blacks in public school classes for the mentally retarded as would be expected from their proportion in the population, and only half as many Anglos as would be expected. The Black and Chicano children in these classes had higher IQ's and fewer physical disabilities than the Anglo children. While we found no evidence that these ethnic disproportions resulted from a conscious policy of discrimination, the labeling process is clearly Anglocentric.

We then sought to identify the aspects of the clinical assessment process that produce ethnic disproportions, by testing a representative sample of 6,907 persons in the community. We used the American Association for Mental Deficiency's definition of mental retardate as a person subaverage in both general intellectual functioning and adaptive behavior and developed a series of 28 age-graded scales to measure adaptive behavior. We also used standardized measures of intelligence, mainly the Stanford-Binet LM and the Kuhlmann-Binet.

We found that the educational institutions' definition of mental retardates as those with IQ's of 79 or below—the lowest 9 percent of the population—is one factor producing ethnic disproportions in the labeling process. We concluded that a 3 percent cutoff—IQ below 70—is most likely to identify persons in need of special assistance and least likely to stigmatize those who perform a normal complement of social roles.

Most psychologists give only an IQ test when making assessments of mental retardation. However, we found that 60 percent of the Chicanos and 91 percent of the Blacks in our sample who had IQ test scores below 70 passed the adaptive behavior measure, while none of the Anglos with IQ's this low were performing normally in their social roles. The IQ test is obviously not a valid predictor of social role performance for Chicanos and Blacks, although it seems to do a good job for Anglos. Schools should adhere to the AAMD definition of mental retardation and develop a systematic method for measuring adaptive behavior as well as IQ in making psychological assessments. A child should have to fail both criteria before being labeled mentally retarded. When we followed this procedure, ethnic disproportions were reduced but still not completely eliminated.

The IQ tests now being used by psychologists are, to a large extent, Anglocentric. We found that about 32 percent of the differences in IQ test scores in a sample of 1,500 Blacks, Chicano, and Anglo elementary school children in California could be accounted for by differences in the sociocultural characteristics of their families. Unfortunately, most psychologists treat a score as a score. When social background was held constant, there was no difference between the measured intelligence of Mexican-American and Black children and the Anglo children on whom the test was

68

standardized. We concluded that diagnostic procedures in the public schools must be broadened to reflect the pluralistic nature of American society and must involve securing information beyond that ordinarily used in public school assessment.

A major concern of parents we interviewed in our studies was the stigmatization of their children. Their children were ashamed to be seen entering the mentally retarded room and dreaded receiving mail that might bear compromising identification. The parents were also concerned about the quality of the educational program in the self-contained special education class. Their children were not taught to read as they would be taught in the regular classes, and many saw the program as a "sentence of death." We followed a group of 108 children in special classes for several years; only one in five ever returned to regular classes. The others aged out, dropped out, or were sent to other special programs.

It would be a tragedy, however, if special education programs were jeopardized because of inadequacies in assessment procedures and programing. I believe that there are viable alternatives to present practices without resorting to dumping special education students and cutting special education funds. School psychologists should be required to enlarge the scope of information they use in making educational decisions by regularly and systematically studying students' adaptive behavior in nonschool situations. If a child performs adequately in these settings, his or her problems are school specific and will need special tutoring, programed learning, cross-age teaching, and remedial reading, rather than a self-contained classroom. School psychologists should also secure information about a child's sociocultural background to use in interpreting his or her IQ test score and developing pluralistic norms. The child's performance should be compared not only with the performance of the general population, which is composed primarily of Anglo children, but also with the performance of other children from his or her own sociocultural background.

I do not agree with those who say we must stop all educational labeling or IQ testing. Our problem has been that our labels are too few and too crude. We need a more sensitive system for identifying children in need of special education and a continuum of special education programs carefully targeted for children with specific needs. One of the most distressing developments in some regions has been the precipitous reassignment of many children to the regular classroom from self-contained classrooms with no continuation of special services. These children must continue to receive special education, and that money must continue to be provided. Financial support and the effort of special education teachers should be redirected toward providing a wider variety of special services to keep children in the educational mainstream and to educate each to his or her maximum potential.

BIAS IN TESTING
by William F. Brazziel

Thousands of minority children are denied equal access to quality education each year because of flaws in the testing apparatus of our schools. This situation, which is both illegal and immoral, is becoming less and less tenable. At least 20 class action suits around the country are seeking to force school districts to cease and desist in the inaccurate testing of minority children. In the biggest suit, in California, the NAACP and several civic groups are seeking a dissolution of classes for the retarded and a moratorium on testing until better, more precise instruments are devised.

The testing problems of minority children begin on the first day at school, when they have to take imprecise tests and have their scores recorded on a cumulative record. Should a child's score be less than 100, the teachers will not work diligently with the child, giving the child less than his or her share of attention and assistance. The child will get more than the ordinary share of slights and indignities as he or she moves through the schools and will be denied access to a college preparatory curriculum.

More and more people are losing confidence in the schools, and the spectacle of a testing apparatus in disarray will do little to restore this confidence. The $300 million testing industry must come up with better instruments. The schools must eliminate injurious instruments, and psychometrists and teachers must be retrained to ensure that tests become a part of the solution rather than the problem in American schools. Resistance to this reform movement will come from long-time test consultants, conservative school people, racists, teachers of teachers, and the psychometric profession.

Henry Dyer, vice-president of the Educational Testing Service and the dean of American psychometrists, says that IQ tests are the most useless source of educational controversy ever invented and that schools which have not yet dropped them should do so forthwith. He notes that a more sophisticated testing apparatus could be developed for schools with a heterogenous population, but that the continuation of IQ tests would preclude this. Dyer is right. The very best test in America was standardized on 4,400 children, most from California suburbs. Neither minority children nor children from the Southeast were included in the sample.

Dyer suggests more school programs based on the philosophy of Jean Piaget. In the Piagetian school, teachers, tests, and curriculum are viewed as resources to maximize each child's development. Instead of being slapped in the face with a biased IQ test, a child takes a battery of sophisticated tests designed to ascertain his or her language development, comprehension, symbol manipulation, discriminant analysis, and other skills. None of the child's scores are recorded in a cumulative folder. Criterion-referenced tests are used instead of the norm-based achievement tests, so child racing is eliminated. In the Piagetian school, parent conferences and skill sheets replace report cards, and continuous progress learning replaces promotion from grade to grade.

Piagetian teachers sometimes give environmental or culture-specific tests, in which familiar concepts from the child's neighborhood are used to ascertain his or her ability to think. A Mississippi child, for example, might be asked to match single-tree, lespedeza, sweetmilk, tedder, dasher, hame-strap, blue tick, and walker, instead of sonata and bas-relief. The content of any test is irrelevant in the Piagetian school.

Culture-specific tests are not new, but the testing corporations have found it unproductive to develop tests for each of the 40 or so cultural groups in this country. The government and the corporations should have such tests available in a few years, but in the meantime school systems and individual teachers will have to make their own. There is no great mystery about test making; over 10,000 tests are on the market. Like the struggle to get publishers to market integrated textbooks, this movement will probably have to resort to teacher and school system efforts to prime the pump.

The situation concerning criterion-referenced tests is better. These achievement tests, which measure only what has been taught—in a particular module, by a particular teacher, and in a particular time span—come with such model programs as

Distar and individually prescribed instruction. Their value lies in their elimination of the need to have losers in the testing game who make it possible for others to succeed. They focus on growth and behaviorally oriented goals and so benefit both low-income and middle class children.

Nothing that is wrong with the testing programs in American schools is immune to hard work, imagination, and nerve. The denial of equal access to quality education is criminal, and the public will not tolerate it. If a few in our midst are resistant to change, we shall find ourselves caught up in an embarrassing maze of court suits, reduced budgets, performance contracts, school vouchers, and steadily eroding public confidence. Our job is to make sure that this does not happen and that American schools are modified to serve well all the children of all the people.

USE OF TESTS: EDUCATIONAL ADMINISTRATION
by Jose A. Cardenas

The purpose of evaluation and testing is decision making. Tests—of intelligence, achievement, and personality—provide information for making decisions about continuation, promotion, graduation, special assignment and placement, diagnosis and prescription, student feedback, motivation, and evaluation. I will focus on the intelligence test.

The most serious problem in the assessment of intelligence and the use of intelligence tests is the assumptions that are made. One assumption is that intelligence is intangible and not directly measurable. Another is that intelligence can be indirectly measured by assessing some form of behavior or performance that is assumed to be solely dependent on intelligence and not related to other variables such as related understandings, prior learnings, and motivation. A third assumption is that the evaluation of behavior and performance requires written, oral, or nonverbal interaction between tester and testee. A fourth is that test results give little or no information unless a comparison is made between the performances of the testee and the norm group. We also assume that the characteristics of the two are compatible.

Research indicates, however, that more is unknown than is known about intelligence and that the assumptions and methods of testing are not always valid. Performance can be based on more than the one variable of intelligence. Our assumption that all other factors are equal or are nondependent variables that have nothing to do with intelligence is false. Language facility, reading ability, and cultural compatibility all influence test scores.

Too many intelligence tests assume that all children have had common experiences, for example, that they are all familiar with snow. We haven't had a snow holiday for the last five years in the Edgewood school district, and most of the kids have never seen snow, yet some group intelligence tests ask about the use of a sled. One question on the WISC asks, "If your mother sends you to the store for a loaf of bread and there is none, what do you do?" The child who answers, "I go back home," is considered to be intellectually inferior to the child who says, "I go to another store." However, in rural areas, there is no place else to go. In some families, the parent and not the child is supposed to make such a decision. During my youth, I was sent for tortillas, and the purchase of a loaf of bread was unheard of in my house until I was 15 years old.

Testing methods can also be incompatible with a culture. For example, some tests emphasize competitiveness, but Mexican American children perform better in a cooperative situation.

Our assumption that an individual has the ability to verbalize can harm children with physical disabilities. A child who stammers will probably score low on a verbal or language test even though this disability is unrelated to the child's intelligence. Motivation is assumed not to be a factor influencing a child's performance on intelligence tests, yet a test may be highly motivating for some children and totally inhibiting for others. We also assume that the testee-tester relationship is not a dependent variable, yet many studies indicate that Black and Mexican American pupils perform better on intelligence tests when they are administered by Black and Mexican American administrators. Score reliability is, likewise, assumed, but how smart you are is more dependent upon who scores your test than upon your intelligence or your performance.

The second major problem in testing is the dysfunctional responses we sometimes use to try to remedy our invalid assumptions. It is simplistic to give a Puerto Rican child a Spanish translation of the WISC or the Peabody Picture Vocabulary Inventory. Some English stimulus words become Spanish paragraphs when translated properly. I have never heard a one-word translation of "cream puff," yet this word is on the Spanish version. Also, the Spanish equivalent of an English word may be on an entirely different level of difficulty. No matter how good the Spanish translation of a test, it must also take into account the regional variation of the language. When I once told a test translator that her translation must be regionalized to be valid, she protested the expense and said, "If the kids don't know this type of Spanish, that's their problem." So Spanish-language tests can be just as invalid as English-language tests for Spanish-speaking children.

Bilingual children who take Spanish-language tests receive no credit for their knowledge of English and, in fact, are penalized. The failure of a bilingual child to respond to the stimulus word *mariposa* supposedly indicates lack of intelligence, even though the child may understand the word and concept of *butterfly*. When bilingual children are administered a Spanish-language Peabody after having taken the English version, they select the same responses they made in English, even though they now see that some of them are wrong. Even using bilingual tests does not solve the problem; scores have been shown to vary according to whether the child's dominant language appears first or second on the page.

We must protect all children against invalid testing. We must reeducate educational personnel and perhaps discontinue intelligence testing, at least until the reeducation is complete. We must develop new and functional techniques for measuring intelligence and establish different criteria for making decisions. Above all, measures should be taken by the National Education Association and organizations of school administrators and counselors to protect children from the invasion of privacy through testing.

USE OF TESTS: EMPLOYMENT AND COUNSELING
by Thelma Spencer

Tests are widely used in counseling, but their validity depends on the interpretation of scores and on the situational appropriateness of the tests. The interpretation of scores often indicates the poor quality of the counseling to which students are exposed.

> ... [A] young girl had received honors in junior high school and top scores in every standardized test she took. As she was about to graduate she was given an interest inventory. According to her responses, the girl's major interest was in clerical work.
>
> The school guidance counselor met with the girl and informed her she should become a secretary. Not only did the counselor tell her she would be happier in a commercial course in high school, he insisted that she would be unable to cope with the intellectual demands of a liberal arts college. In his ignorance the guidance counselor had confused a questionnaire that supposedly shows what people *like* to do with aptitude tests that attempt to measure what people *can* do.[1]

Bad counseling can take other forms, as in this incident related by a New York high school student:

> ... [T]he people in my section were never told about the PSATs. ... The kids in the Honor sections took those PSATs as a matter of course. In fact, the teachers strongly urged that they take those PSATs in order to get some practice for the next year's SATs. And I didn't take a PSAT until I got into my senior year, and then I found out I had to take an SAT.
>
> That sticks in my craw. We were all students and we supposedly were all aspiring to college.[2]

In both of these cases the system worked against the student, but the first student is representative of the type for whom the system is supposed to work. The second is representative of those for whom the system works very seldom.

Tests also mediate against students. Some children are tested more than they are taught and curriculum is often based on what can be measured by existing instruments. Too many counselors equate a test score with the intangibles of personality—motivation, desire, and ambition—and then ignore personality in favor of a preconceived notion about the individual being counseled. "The best of our tests," as Oscar Buros says, "are still highly fallible instruments which are extremely difficult to interpret with assurance in individual cases."[3] Many counselors and teachers victimize youngsters by equating the individual with the norm and the testee group with the norm group.

Some people say that the evolution of a stable examination system has helped create our much vaunted stable education system, but while the SAT may permit admissions officers to select students most similar to the norm group, those students come from schools whose programs are based on what the colleges offer. The implications of this vicious circle are staggering: too many poor and minority students who fail to meet admissions criteria are guided into general, vocational, and commercial classes.

Sometimes a student succeeds despite a counselor's or teacher's doubts about his or her ability to do so. Many students never even see a counselor, or if they do, the counselor is a disciplinarian and attendance taker, not a helper and adviser. For the majority of students, adequate counseling and guidance are myths.

Using test scores to determine employability is another gross misuse of tests. For example, the National Teacher Examinations have been used by some to determine who should be retained when a southern school district is under court order to dissolve its dual system. When the school system in Columbus, Mississippi, required a cutoff score of 1,000 on the NTE for retention in the unified district, eight Black teachers were not rehired. In Starkville, Mississippi, the school district used the Graduate Record Examination to determine teacher retention, although it granted provisional status to teachers with NTE scores of 500 on both the common and teaching field sections. These districts equated a test score with competence in the classroom. In April 1971 Judge Orma Smith ruled that personnel selection based on NTE and GRE results was discriminatory, as more whites than Blacks scored above the cutoff point in both districts. In *Griggs et al. v. Duke Power Company* the U.S. Supreme Court ruled that tests for employability violate the 1964 Civil Rights Act "when the rate of rejection is higher for Negroes than for whites and there is no showing that the passing of such tests is significantly related to the successful performance of the job."

Test scores are guides only, and the NTE score is merely another piece—by no means the most important piece—of information about a person. This test, or any test, is only as good as the people who use it.

MISUSE OF TESTS: SELF-CONCEPT
by Robert L. Williams

The problem of testing Black children is very serious. Biased tests are not just a violation of civil rights, but are a form of Black intellectual genocide. The whole American educational system is unfair, and the argument against tests is used as one instrument to open the door to change the whole system.

What do we mean by intelligence? Is it what the intelligence tests measure? Is it a global capacity to deal with one's environment? I offer the rubber band theory to illustrate my definition of intelligence. A rubber band will stay in its relaxed state unless stretched to its capacity by an outside force. Genetics or heredity determines an individual's potential stretch, and the environment determines the extent to which he or she reaches this potential.

Test items drawn from white culture penalize Black children, whereas items drawn from Black culture penalize whites. I have developed the BITCH test—Black Intelligence Test of Cultural Homogeneity—with items drawn directly from Black culture. A child who knows Malcolm X's birthday or the date of his assassination shows as much intelligence as the one who knows Washington's birthday. I've never seen the work *pick* illustrated on the WISC—only *comb*, which is something I can't use.

The three criteria for a test—validity, reliability, and standardization—exclude Black people. A test is valid when it measures what it intends to measure. Currently used ability tests do not measure Black intelligence. If a test asks, for example, "What should you do if you find a purse with five dollars in it?" Black children will say, "Keep it"—a culturally determined response. They will say what their environment has dictated that they say, but on the standardized test, they will be marked zero.

Reliability means test consistency, i.e., a test will yield the same score or rank an individual in the same place each time. Since the standardized tests are scored subjectively, and since they validate only mainstream cultural responses, they cannot be reliable.

Standardization refers to the extent to which the sample on which the test is based represents the people who will take it. Several of the major ability tests excluded Blacks, Mexican Americans, and Puerto Ricans from their standardization samples. The Stanford-Binet, WISC, and Peabody systematically excluded Blacks from their samples. If a test is not standardized on a particular group, it probably does not represent that particular group and should not be used on its members. Standardization is one reason for the 15-point difference in IQ between Black and white kids. The discrepancy means simply that the test is biased.

Arthur Jensen's research has repeatedly shown that tests are biased—that Black and Chicano kids who have IQ's in the 60-to-80 range score much higher on Learning Tests than do white kids with the same IQ. Jensen's interpretation is that Blacks show more associative or Level I learning than whites; if you ask Black and white kids to recite six digits backwards and forwards, Black kids do better than whites with the same IQ. An alternative interpretation is that the biased IQ underestimates the ability of Black children and indicates that they are clearly superior to the white kids who scored within the same range on the test, because the test was standardized on the whites.

Some people argue, "The tests do exactly what they are supposed to do. They predict scholastic success." Ability tests (X) predict a criterion (Y), such as a child's performance in the classroom. The hidden fallacy is variable Z, which might be unfairness, motivation, anxiety—anything that influences X (test scores). A fair test and a fair criterion will produce a high correlation between X and Y: white people who do well on tests do well in school. The unfair WISC and a fair classroom will produce a low correlation between X and Y: a Black child who does poorly on the test will do well in the classroom. Another combination is a fair predictor, such as the Davis-Eels Games test, and an unfair criterion—the culturally biased classroom. This combination will also yield a low correlation: Black kids will do well on the test and poorly in the classroom. With an unfair predictor and an unfair criterion—the classic situation for the Black child—the correlation is high: the Black child who does poorly on the test also does poorly in the classroom.

After I administered the WISC test to about 500 Black kids, I then gave the BITCH test. Of the 420 children in the low WISC group, 75 to 80 percent scored high on the BITCH. I still have to examine other criteria to see how well the BITCH scores correlate with scholastic performance, but at least I know that most of the Black children who scored low on the WISC are neither educationally mentally retarded nor in the borderline defective range.

At least four court suits are now pending on the use of standardized tests in San Francisco, San Diego, Boston, and St. Louis because they violate a child's constitutional rights under the Fourteenth Amendment.

The Boehm's test of 50 basic concepts is clearly written for white folks. It asks the child to select the picture that shows "behind the couch" or "under the table." A Black child does not say "behind" but "in back of"—not "under" but "up under." We are now rewriting the instructions to that test to see if children understand the concepts in Black English. Black and white children can have the same cognition but communicate it differently. To the cognition "few," a Black child might say, "Well, that's not a whole bunch of them." Only the vocabulary is different, and a difference is not a deficiency. You don't evaluate Black people in terms of how white they are, but this is what the tests have done. They do not measure Black ability.

Eliminating and inhibiting intelligence early in life is the best way to keep Blacks out of the system. I would opt for talking to children in the dialect they understand. If a child can understand what you are asking of him or her on a test, that child will probably master the task. You cannot expect an individual who has not been exposed to German or French to understand these languages. This does not mean that he or she lacks the capacity to learn German or French, but that the child lacks that particular exposure.

Black parents should be concerned about both the predictive variable, the test, and the criterion variable, the classroom. I think whites should also be vitally concerned. Brother Charlie Mingus said, "When they came and took the Catholics, I did not complain, because I am not a Catholic. When they came and took the Unionists, I did not complain, because I am not a Unionist. When they came and took the Panthers, I did not complain, because I am not a Panther, but then one day they came and took me." I don't think we should let another generation pass in this country that knows all about extra-vehicular space activity, atomic physics, and all of these highfalutin things, but does not know what a human being is.

THE S.H.A.F.T.* TEST

A highlight of the conference was the participation of more than 40 high school students, who reacted to the speakers, joined in the discussion groups, and wrote and administered the S.H.A.F.T. test.

The students from Callanan Junior High School in Des Moines, Iowa, told conference participants to keep their tests face down until told to start. They would be given 10 minutes to answer 22 multiple choice questions about student culture that were standardized on ninth grade students from Des Moines. Student proctors enforced the no-talking, no-peeking rules, although from time to time the educators asked for erasers, wanted to know the time, and called out, "Hey, Teach! Where's the pencil sharpener?"

The test scores formed a perfect bell-shaped curve—a handful of the 650 conferees scored high, most were average, and a few below it. Besides the public exposure—conferees had to wear black, red, or yellow armbands depending on their scores, or go bare armed for scoring too low—participants were told that their scores would be made part of their cumulative folders to haunt them for life.

(Student's Hype Arranged for Teachers)

1. What is the slang word used to describe a blemish?
   a. Zilch
   b. Arg
   c. Zit

2. The author of the book *Right On* is
   a. Julian Bond
   b. Jerry Rubin
   c. Iman Baraka (LeRoi Jones)

3. What are waffle stompers?
   a. Pancake chef
   b. Snowshoes
   c. Ice cream sandwiches

4. *Steal This Book* was written by
   a. Allen Ginsberg
   b. Eldridge Cleaver
   c. Abbie Hoffman

5. Who wrote the song "Purple Haze"?
   a. Jimi Hendrix
   b. Aretha Franklin
   c. James Brown

6. For what purpose would you use a roach clip?
   a. To keep ladies' blouses closed
   b. To hold the end of a reefer
   c. To get rid of bugs

7. Who wrote *Love Story?*
   a. Ryan O'Neal
   b. Henry Mancini
   c. Erich Segal

8. The author of *Alice's Restaurant* is
   a. Bob Dylan
   b. Alice Cooper
   c. Arlo Guthrie

9. What can you get at "Alice's Restaurant"?
   a. Soul food
   b. Storybooks for children
   c. Everything you want

10. "Ripple" is
    a. Rumor in a faculty
    b. Cheap wine
    c. A game of chance

11. The term *rip off* means
    a. To tear
    b. To steal
    c. To cop out

12. What rock group sang the anti-drug song, "The Pusher"?
    a. The Who
    b. Steppenwolf
    c. Blood Rock

13. "Tommy" is
    a. A British cop
    b. A fast sports car
    c. A rock opera

*S.H.A.F.T. stands for "Student's Hype Arranged for Teachers."

78

14. "Make tracks" means
    a. To inject dope
    b. To burn rubber
    c. To split

15. To "crash" is to
    a. Have an accident
    b. Come down from the use of drugs
    c. Lose all your money

16. Who were the originators of *Jesus Christ Superstar?*
    a. Rado & Ragni
    b. Rice & Webber
    c. Brewer & Shipley

17. *Lenny* is a play on the life of
    a. Lenny Bruce
    b. Lenny Bernstein
    c. Lenny Brezhnev

18. "Getting off" means
    a. To feel the effect from the drugs you have taken
    b. A vacation from work
    c. To cease the addiction of heroin

19. A "hit" is
    a. A robbery
    b. An internal dose of drugs
    c. A very popular teenager

20. Hash is
    a. Cheap opium
    b. A mixture of pep pills
    c. A resin from marijuana

21. A "hemmie" is
    a. A souped-up engine
    b. An Ernest Hemingway short story
    c. A shirt that has been shortened

22. An ounce of marijuana is referred to as a
    a. Reefer
    b. Key
    c. Lid

—Written and administered by students from Callanan Junior High School, Des Moines, Iowa

Key to S.H.A.F.T. Test

1. c	9. c	16. b
2. b	10. b	17. a
3. b	11. b	18. a
4. c	12. b	19. b
5. a	13. c	20. c
6. b	14. a	21. a
7. c	15. b	22. c
8. c		

How To Score

0- 4 correct—Nothing
5-10 correct—Yellow armband
11-16 correct—Red armband
17-22 correct—Black armband

WRAP-UP
by Dwight Allen

Testing is a part of the mindless process of education that really is suited to the simpler society of the past. Education is out of date sociologically, psychologically, and physiologically, but I would rather work within the system than burn it down. Either way, traumatic change will hurt people—by and large, the wrong people. If you were to close down all the educational systems in this country, the people in the upper middle-class would pretty much do it on their own, but the people who most need to gain access to education would be done in.

This doesn't mean that you shouldn't do in a particular test, because some need to be done in. For example, if you are like most audiences, only about 20 percent of you can name the capitals of North and South Dakota and North and South Carolina—except for the fifth grade teachers. The real standard for an educated person is not being able to name states and their capitals but being able to use an atlas to find them when one needs to. When I suggested to a fifth grade teacher that she let her kids use an atlas on the next test, she said, "Oh, no! You couldn't do that. They'd all get it right."

Our whole testing program is oriented toward a normative assumption—an upper and a lower half. I won't buy into any system that requires someone to fall off the bottom, bacause this isn't my view of what education is about. An educational system is needed that will assure a win/win proposition for children instead of the present zero/win game.

Very few of us in education ever know when we're done, despite all the tests we give. If a student seems about finished, we enrich him or her, and in the name of high standards we go about it all backwards. Kids soon learn that rewards are given not for achievement, but for keeping the seat warm, being good, and working hard. If a kid comes in with a theme, throws it on the teacher's desk, and says, "Here's something I whipped off in 20 minutes. I hope you like it," the teacher says, "You should have worked harder." If the same kid

brings in the same paper and says, "Here's the eighth draft. I wish I had time for a ninth," she says, "Nice boy, Johnny. You are working hard."

A revitalization of the testing program has to be thought of in terms of the broader objectives of education. The problem with this, however, is that anytime people want to avoid having to do something, they say, "Let's stop and get our objectives organized." This is good for at least two years. My objectives are the same as yours. I want all the kids to be constructive members of society, to be self-realized and have lots of skills, and to be happy, healthy, and democratic. The objective of our school system, however, is status. With so many people being anointed first with high school diplomas and now with college degrees, it's getting hard to make that status system stick. Education should reflect a status system that is based on legitimate differences in ability.

Here is an example of the nonnormative kind of education I think we ought to have. Graduate education students at UCLA have to take "Statistics for Teachers." Assume that this course is necessary and that the objective is to make students learn it better. The course is divided into 16 units, each one lasting a week. The first unit is called "Counting." The students start out in large groups, enter supplementary groups, and then join small tutorial sessions, not quitting until they have learned the week's work. They are tested as soon as they learn the material—some after the first hour and others after 15 hours. In the typical college course, students take a midterm at the end of about the fifth week. This is the first chance teachers get to find out what their students are learning. Those for whom the instruction hasn't worked are five weeks behind before anybody gets the first inkling. Tests come at the wrong time, but as long as the system has enough people clinking out at the end, we are not bothered about those who are ground up inside. The "Statistics for Teachers" course produces between 85 and 90 percent A's, proving that anybody can learn almost anything that we teach in school. I am not sure that we are serving anybody, however, by reorganizing a system that's already no good and out of phase with what society needs.

The number one priority for every program in the School of Education at the University of Massachusetts is to combat institutional racism. Our admissions procedure produces a bimodal population of students—the Ivy League-Phi Beta Kappa type in one hump, and in the other, the people who are just smart. We talk to prospective students and admit the ones we like. When we get through with them, no can tell the two groups apart anymore. This is very necessary if you are eliminating a testing program, for you should never patronize the folks at the bottom by giving them a second-class education. We also think that writing dissertations does not indicate leadership in education and that not all doctoral candidates—whether Ivy League or non-Ivy League types—should have to write dissertations. My point is to find a *different* standard and apply it to *all* students.

One of the problems with testing is that it permits decisions only about individuals and never about institutions. I would like to use testing and evaluation to help me make decisions about our program, but I need information about the experiences that contribute to educational competence and leadership. We offer 16 programs, some self-contained with no core requirements, some that are totally touchy-feely, and others that are dice-them-up-and-competency-base-them. Each can succeed on its own terms and is allowed to do so. We must find out what is good for whom and for what. Aptitude treatment interaction may help us. We also have to begin to look at subcultural differences in a different way to find a unity within a diversity, to appreciate being different, to make our educational system reflect this, and to find standards and ways of checking up that are free of the insidious by-products that the testing program has given us. I want to test the people who can learn from tests and prohibit testing the people for whom learning is obstructed by tests.

This society will never succeed until we recognize that we are part of a multiracial, multiclass, multisex world. We must develop strategies to make people produce on their own good intentions. There must be a renovation of testing and curriculum and an end to the idea that teachers are neutral. So long as teachers have to pretend to be objective, so long as schools can teach only those things that are safe for everybody, education will be unreal. We are living in a complex world, and our school system has to become complex.

REPORT OF THE NEA TASK FORCE ON TESTING, 1975

INTRODUCTION

This report is submitted to the 1975 Representative Assembly by the Task Force on Testing in fulfillment of its responsibilities under New Business Items 51 and 28, adopted by the 1972 Assembly, which stated:

The NEA shall establish a task force to deal with numerous and complex problems communicated to it under the general heading of testing. This task force shall report its findings and proposals for further action at the 1973 Representative Assembly. (Item 1972-51)

This Representative Assembly directs the National Education Association to immediately call a national moratorium on standardized testing and at the same time set up a task force on standardized testing to research and make its findings available to the 1975 Representative Assembly for further action. (Item 1972-28)

In the report of its findings to the 1973 Representative Assembly the Task Force set down some well-founded beliefs which have drawn a significant amount of attention from both inside and outside the profession. Follow-up efforts served to further verify and intensify the positions taken. The Task Force feels, therefore, that the most appropriate final report it can make to the 1975 Representative Assembly is a reinforcement and redeclaration of those beliefs, with recommendations to the Association (a) to make them the basis for future NEA policy on testing issues and (b) to continue seeking, through appropriate program and other efforts, ways of countering widespread misuse and abuses in educational and psychological testing as they relate to teachers and students, particularly those who are culturally and linguistically different.

The Task Force also addresses itself here to matters which have added weight to its stated beliefs—to important court actions, some of which involve the united teaching profession; to the valuable liaisons it has established with other groups; to special writings developed for use by the Task Force; to supportive literature; and to the moratorium issue.

The Task Force is indebted to the many persons who contribute their expertise to its total three-year effort through personal or indirect testimony, consultation, or other assistance, and to those who have taken notice of its findings.

This report was approved by the NEA Task Force on Testing at its final meeting on April 5, 1975, by unanimous vote of the members present.

TASK FORCE POSITIONS AND CONSIDERATIONS

As stated in its first interim report and as strengthened in further deliberation on the issues, the NEA Task Force on Testing believes:[1]

1. *That some measurement and evaluation in education is necessary.*
2. *That some of the measurement and evaluation tools developed over the years, and currently in use, contain satisfactory validity and reliability requirements and serve useful purposes when properly administered and interpreted.*
3. *That certain measurement and evaluation tools are either invalid and unreliable, out of date, or unfair and should be withdrawn from use.*
4. *That the training of those who use measurement and evaluation tools is woefully inadequate and that schools of education, school systems, the education profession, and the testing industry all must take responsibility for correcting these inadequacies. Such training must develop understanding about the limitations of tests in predicting potential learning ability, about their lack of validity in measuring innate characteristics, and their dehumanizing effects on many students. It must also develop understanding of students' rights related to testing and the use of test results.*
5. *That there is overkill in the use of tests and that the intended purposes of testing can be accomplished through the use of individual diagnostic instruments, through sampling techniques which involve the use of tests, and through a variety of alternatives to tests.*
6. *That the National Teacher Examinations are an improper tool and must not be used for teacher certification, recertification, selection,*

84

assignment, retention, salary determination, promotion, transfer, tenure, or dismissal.

7. *That no test results should be used as a basis for allocation of federal, state, or local funds.*

8. *That no tests should be used for tracking students.*

9. *That while the purposes and procedures of the National Assessment of Education may have been initially sound, a number of state adaptations of the program—in Michigan[2] and New Jersey, for example—have subverted the original intent and as a result are harmful.*

10. *That both the content and the use of the typical group intelligence test are biased against those who are economically disadvantaged and culturally and linguistically different. In fact, group intelligence tests are potentially harmful to all students.*

11. *That the use of the typical intelligence test contributes to what has come to be termed "the self-fulfilling prophecy," whereby students' achievement tends to fulfill the expectations held by others.*

12. *That test results are often used by educators, students, and parents in ways that are damaging to the self-concept of many students.*

13. *That the testing industry must demonstrate significantly increased responsibility for validity, reliability, and relevance of their tests, for their fair application, and for accurate and just interpretation and use of the results.*

14. *That the public, and some in the profession, misinterpret the results of tests as they relate to status and needs of groups of students as well as to individual students.*

15. *That the overemphasis in assessment programs on testing recall-type, cognitive facts has tended to shift teaching emphasis to tasks which are simple and easy to measure and has resulted in serious inattention to the complex, higher-level mental processes and to affective skills and attitudes which are so difficult to measure but which are equally and, in some respects, more important.*

In summary, the Task Force believes:

That the major use of tests should be to improve instruction—to diagnose learning dif-

ficulties and to plan learning activities in response to learning needs. Tests must not be used in any way to label and classify students, to track students into homogeneous groups, to determine educational programs, to perpetuate an elitism, or to maintain some groups and individuals "in their place" near the bottom of the socioeconomic ladder. In short, tests must not be used in ways that will deny any student full access to equal educational opportunity.

Some Special Considerations

EFFECTS OF TESTS ON MINORITIES

Throughout its study the Task Force has been especially impressed with the depth of feeling and the weight of evidence against group standardized tests as reliable/valid measures of achievement and intelligence. Throughout its stated beliefs it has alluded to the injurious and prejudicial aspects of such tests. The term *standardized* implies homogeneity, stereotyping, and equalized development and achievement, and is contradictory to the best interests of a pluralistic society. The practice of standardized testing has, in fact, deprived minorities—the economically disadvantaged, culturally and linguistically different, and women—access to equal educational opportunity.

Traditional IQ testing particularly has come under increasingly heavy attack for falsely labeling many minority children as "mentally retarded," based on what Jane Mercer has termed Anglo-centric measures.[3] Such tests are touted as reliable/valid measures of the ability and achievement of varying populations even though the test-takers' educational and cultural backgrounds, opportunities, and experiences may be markedly different from those on whom the tests are standardized.

Recently, Robert L. Green, educational psychologist and dean of the College of Urban Development at Michigan State University, called intelligence testing "the awesome danger" and pointed to the potential compounding of that danger by continued use of traditional IQ tests:

... experiences of black and other minority children are not reflected in the content of the test. This bias is even more apparent when the child's opportunities have been limited due to poverty. Consequently, many black children start test-taking with a good chance of "flunking" an "experience" they have never been exposed to . . . . When a child is labeled as a "ne'er-do-well" in the early grades and is forced to keep wearing that label, important educational opportunities are denied him. Sometimes he may never be taught to read; he certainly will not be given access to college preparation courses. Discrimination in education means disadvantage in the job market. A low-paying job means low-income status—so a test victim's children may become test victims themselves.[4]

Widespread dissemination of test results which can be easily misinterpreted, cases of invasion of privacy, and proposals for educational funding on the basis of test scores add further evidence of the potential harmfulness of standardized testing.

The Task Force restates emphatically that since currently used standardized tests in general are developed and normed for students of Anglo-American middle-class culture and economic status, any use of the results of standardized testing to place or track students, to denigrate minority intelligence, to discriminate against groups or individuals, to restrict funding of programs, or to misinform the public constitutes deplorable practice and denies access to equal opportunity.

The Task Force calls for a humanistic approach to student evaluation on the part of all those who have a role and responsibility in the process. In particular:

- The Task Force urges teachers
  - to develop understanding of their students' socioeconomic backgrounds and sensitivity to their individual needs and problems

  - to refuse to administer tests which they find to be biased

  - to secure by appropriate means their right to be involved in school and school district decision making related to testing

  - to exert collective influence on the testing industry and on state and local school systems in order to secure from

them a firm commitment to evaluation programs, the purpose of which is not to compare students but to improve instruction.

- The Task Force urges spokespersons of all cultures to continue exposing erroneous contentions that some groups in society are genetically less intelligent than others.

- The Task Force urges the testing industry to take greatly increased responsibility for turning out fair and bias-free tests and for constantly monitoring the distribution and application of their products to ensure proper use.

- The Task Force urges education agencies at all levels to institute sampling procedures for all large-scale assessments, the results of which should be used for general information purposes only.

COURT ACTIONS

Years of controversy over testing practices has also led to civil suits. The continued use of tests in teacher licensure and hiring and continued use of biased instruments with students who are disadvantaged and culturally and linguistically different increase the possibilities for legal action against school systems and the almost unregulated testing industry.

In 1971 the Supreme Court ruled in *Griggs v. Duke Power Co.* that tests given to job applicants had to be job-related. This case has been cited in court decisions related to standardized testing of teachers. It was referred to, for example, in the 1974 decision in favor of 13 Black teachers against the school board of Nansemond County, Virginia, as were arguments presented by the NEA in an amicus curiae brief. The Fourth Circuit Court of Appeals ruled unconstitutional a hiring requirement that teachers take the National Teacher Examinations (NTE) and achieve a minimum score on the common examination. The effect of the requirement was to substantially diminish the Black teaching force. The ruling overturned the trial court's conclusion that the test had content validity, noting that no evidence was presented which established a relationship between questions on the test and knowledge required for teaching, and that it was arbitrary to apply a general knowledge test to teachers of different subjects because their jobs are substantially different.

The Nansemond case is likely to have positive impact on pending litigation in North Carolina in which the united teaching profession is involved. The NEA and the state affiliate have intervened in a Justice Department suit challenging the validity of state requirements for minimum NTE scores for certification purposes which affect both employment and placement on salary scales. In South Carolina, the state education association has filed a complaint under Title VII of the Civil Rights Act of 1964 challenging the use of minimum NTE scores for certification. A favorable decision in a current Georgia suit could eliminate the NTE requirement for advanced certification and its potential restrictions on promotion and pay.

A precedential award in Association-supported litigations, including two major cases involving teacher test requirements, was announced early in 1975. A federal court in Mississippi ordered two school districts in that state to pay $106,000 in attorney fees, expenses, and court costs in cases in which it was alleged and determined that racial discrimination had played a part in employment decisions during a period of desegregation. One of the cases was brought on behalf of a group of Columbus teachers who were fired for failing to achieve minimum scores on the NTE; another case involved a group in Starkville who challenged required scores on the Graduate Record Examinations (GRE). Most of the teachers had previously won the right to reinstatement with back pay.

The NEA and the New Jersey Education Association are challenging that state's assessment program in order to prevent dissemination of standardized test scores which might violate civil and constitutional rights of both teachers and students, and cause racial and ethnic polarization by permitting degrading stigmatization and illegal classifications. The complaint has so far resulted in action by the State Board of Education to remove an ambiguous section of the administrative code that could have been interpreted to permit using test results in conjunction with other data to support

disciplinary action against teachers.

Hobson v. Hansen (1967), in which the court abolished the track system in the District of Columbia public schools, was probably the landmark case tying standardized testing to denial of equal educational opportunity, in this instance to Black and economically disadvantaged students. More recently, two cases still in the courts in California are seeking to uphold the constitutional rights of culturally and linguistically different minority students by preventing the use of standardized IQ tests. The judge, the same in both cases, has found that standardized IQ testing causes a disproportionately high percentage of minority students to be placed in classes for the educable mentally retarded (EMR). In the case of *Diana v. the State Board of Education,* involving Chicano students, a stipulation was issued ordering local boards to come up with a formula to reduce the variance between the percentage of Chicano children in EMR classes and the percentage in the general school population; planning is still under way between the local school systems and the State Department of Education. The case of *Larry P. v. Riles,* brought on behalf of Black students, led to court-ordered stoppage of IQ testing of Black students in the state. The economic factor inherent in recent legislation making IQ testing in California optional at school district expense may also have tended to halt the practice with all students in some places.

LIAISONS

The initiating of dialogues with other organizations and agencies involved with test development, use, and research must be considered an important accomplishment of the Task Force. And it would be in the best interest of practitioners for the Association to continue the dialogues and to establish cooperative working relationships toward the goal of eliminating test misuse and abuse.

Standards Development Groups

The Task Force continues to be concerned over the lack of direct teacher involvement in the formulation of testing standards; for example, the

American Psychological Association's (APA) *Standards for Educational and Psychological Testing.* These standards were developed by a joint committee of the APA, the American Educational Research Association (AERA), and the National Council on Measurement in Education (NCME). The Task Force pursued its concern informally with APA staff and followed up with a request to the APA Board of Directors to approve the inclusion of an NEA representative on the joint committee, which is launching a project to develop guidelines on evaluation of school programs. In a letter to APA, the Task Force chairperson said that "such representation should also explicitly provide that the NEA representatives be involved on a continuing basis with the group and any other group which may be constituted to give continuing direction to, substance and editorial advice on, and make decisions about acceptance, publication, and distribution of such guidelines." No action had been taken on that request at the writing of this report.

Testing Industry

In March 1974 the Task Force formally expressed its disappointment that the Educational Testing Service (ETS) had delayed enforcement of a cut-off in reporting NTE scores to South Carolina because they were being used for purposes of teacher certification, which even ETS considers a misuse of the test. The Task Force notes here that the enforcement was later effected, and commends the ETS action (and reiterates that the united teaching profession is presently seeking to eliminate the South Carolina requirement). The Task Force also welcomes ETS's recent expression of interest in the Task Force beliefs and its initiation of a meeting early in 1975 with NEA and New Jersey staff representatives and the Task Force chairperson to discuss common concerns.

Federal Government

With project funding by the National Institute of Education (NIE) in mind, the Task Force was anxious to learn what is being done at the federal level to encourage research which could have posi-

tive impact on the future of testing. NIE spokespersons conferred with the Task Force and revealed that some projects already approved for funding reflect some of the Task Force concerns.

In this instance, also, the Task Force has broached the subject of teacher representation in those decisions which will affect their practice. Though it is aware that the work of NIE is in the public interest, the Task Force has registered its concern that the public interest will not be well served unless substantial numbers of teachers are represented in NIE goal setting and suggested that the Association be invited to appoint practitioners to all NIE panels. Rather than direct involvement, however, some NIE personnel seem to see NEA's role as lobbyist in the legislative process of defining parameters of NIE responsibility. Such indirect and after-the-fact involvement will continue to be unacceptable to teachers.

Another question put to the NIE spokespersons had to do with the Institute's interest in the establishment of a national center for certifying tests. The response was that at this time the extent of such interest probably would be in exploring the possibilities of such a center. This, of course, is the focus of a current NEA staff study described below.

The Task Force last year informed NEA Government Relations of their concern over the Quie amendment to the then pending H.R. 69 (revision of the Elementary and Secondary Education Act) which proposed to tie educational funding to testing. It was pleased to learn that its concern was relayed and may have been a factor in the withdrawal of that amendment. The issue is now under formal study by both NIE and the General Accounting Office.

NEA FEASIBILITY STUDY FOR TEST CERTIFICATION

Although the Task Force fulfills its official responsibility with this report, it views a parallel staff assignment as an extention of its work and wants the general membership to be aware of it. Staff in the Professional Excellence goal area are currently conducting a study "to determine the feasibility of a system whereby the NEA certifies tests or other procedures for student or program evaluation" (Subobjective 1.4). Three Task Force members also serve on the nine-member advisory committee which is engineering the study.[5] At this writing the committee has established some useful contacts—with the APA, the UCLA Center for the Study of Evaluation, the National Council of Teachers of English, and the National Association of Elementary School Principals. It has drafted a rationale for NEA certifying tests and the appropriate uses of tests, has outlined alternative strategies, and plans a field survey for the final quarter of FY 1974-75 to obtain reactions to the proposed procedure.

SPECIAL PAPERS

During its tenure the Task Force on Testing has initiated work on written statements to support and elaborate on some of its expressed beliefs. Various drafts of these papers have already been cited and utilized in some quarters both inside and outside the profession. All members of the Association should be aware of their existence. Three of the papers are in final form and are published in this report. They are:

1. "Roles and Responsibilities of Groups Concerned with Student Evaluation Systems." This statement directs to specific groups recommendations which the Task Force considers essential for achieving the goals of sound and fair development of tests, their appropriate distribution and administration, accurate and fair interpretation of results, and relevant and constructive action based on the results. The groups addressed are teachers and their associations, other professional associations, students, minorities, the testing industry, school administrators, higher education, and government agencies.
2. "Why Should All Those Students Take All Those Tests?" This paper reflects the Task Force's opinions on random and matrix sampling as opposed to blanket testing. It incorporates material developed by Dr. Frank B. Womer of the Michigan School Testing Service, University of Michigan, on determining the use of sampling procedures.
3. "Guidelines and Cautions for Considering Criterion-Referenced Testing." The concept of criterion-referenced testing (also termed objectives-referenced testing) has been pro-

moted as potentially more useful than norm-referenced testing for measuring learning outcomes for the purpose of improving instruction. This paper attempts to define the criterion-referenced concept and to clear up some of the confusion which surrounds it. Fifteen caveats are listed and discussed. A glossary of measurement terms is appended.

Two other important statements which have been outlined require expertise that is beyond the time and capabilities of the Task Force in order to give them the highest credibility. These have been incorporated into and will be completed as products in the goal area, Professional Excellence.

1. "Some Potential Alternatives to Standardized Tests for Evaluating Student Progress and Diagnosing Learning Needs." Alternatives include criterion- or objectives-referenced tests, oral presentations by students, individual diagnostic tests, group diagnostic tests, teacher-made tests, student self- and peer-evaluation, open admissions, school letter grades, subjective evaluation by teachers, contracts with students, interviews, parent-teacher conferences, student narratives, student products, and actual student performance. This collection has promise as a handbook for teachers.
2. A unit or module for preservice and in-service teacher education pertaining to testing has thus far been outlined in two forms: schema and guidelines. This project stems from concern over the present inadequacy of training as expressed in the Task Force's belief No. 4 (see p. 83).

The Task Force sees all of the above as having potential, collectively, as an NEA "awareness kit" on testing issues.

SUPPORTIVE LITERATURE

The Task Force was impressed with much of the vast amount of literature that has been published on testing and its effects, and considers it appropriate to cite here a few recent items which influenced the formulation of Task Force beliefs or which support some of them. (Citations of other important resources will be found in previous Task Force reports.)

REFERENCES

Blachford, Jean S. "A Teacher Views Criterion-Referenced Tests." *Today's Education* 64: 36; March-April 1975. Points teachers must consider as they "become part of the national movement toward criterion-referenced tests," and a plea for proper in-service education.

De Avila, Edward A., and Havassy, Barbara. "The Testing of Minority Children: A Neo-Piagetian Approach." *Today's Education* 63: 72-75; November-December 1974. A challenge to industry's attempts at restructuring present tests to produce bias-free instruments, and descriptions of an alternative assessment model and a computerized system for use of test data both for general information and to individualize instruction.

Gartner, Alan; Greer, Colin; and Riessman, Frank, editors. *The New Assaults on Equality: IQ and Social Stratification.* New York: Perennial Library (paperback), Harper & Row, 1974. 225 pp. Nine experts examine the past and present of the IQ controversy and draw some important conclusions about the role of IQ in society.

Goslin, David A. *Teachers and Testing.* New York: Russell Sage Foundation, 1967. 201 pp. An exploratory study of the uses of standardized tests in schools, teachers' experience with tests and testing, their attitudes and roles.

Green, Donald Ross. *Racial and Ethnic Bias in Test Construction.* Monterey, Calif.: McGraw-Hill, n.d. Adapted from a federally funded study of the same title. The researcher found the need for changes in test construction procedures to produce unbiased instruments and suggests that research should be a standard part of producing a test.

Holmen, Milton G., and Docter, Richard. *Educational and Psychological Testing.* New York: Russell Sage Foundation, 1972. 218 pp. An evaluative study of the testing industry, its products, and how they are used, with action recommendations for "those who influence the gatekeepers in our society."

Mercer, Jane R. *Labeling the Mentally Retarded.* Berkeley: University of California Press, 1973. Federally sponsored study of "Clinical and Social System Perspectives on Mental Retardation" in an American community. In a popularized description of the study (see "IQ: The Lethal Label," in *Psychology Today* 6: 44-47, 95-97; September 1972), Mercer says that "schools seem to have the primary responsibility for identifying the mentally retarded" via the IQ test, which she concludes is inaccurate and unfair.

National Education Association. *Evaluation and Reporting of Student Achievement.* What Research Says to the Teacher series. Washington, D.C.: the Association, 1974. 32 pp. Review of selected research and literature on (a) purposes of evaluation and reporting, (b) their development in relation to different educational philosophies and teaching methods, (c) the best way to report achievement, and (d) evaluation to improve instruction.

Stiggins, Richard J. "An Alternative to Blanket Standardized Testing." *Today's Education* 64: 38-40; March-April 1975. An explanation of and argument for depending on random and matrix sampling in education testing.

Weber, George. *Uses and Abuses of Standardized Testing in the Schools.* Occasional Papers, No. 22. Washington, D.C.: Council for Basic Education, 1974. 38 pp. Brief, clearly written critique of intelligence, aptitude, and achievement tests; their uses, limitations, and abuses; and discussion of current controversies surrounding standardized testing.

RECOMMENDATIONS

The Task Force recommends that:

1. The Association incorporate the principles inherent in the stated beliefs of the Task Force on Testing in any and all future official NEA policy on testing of students and teachers and the uses of tests and their results.

2. The Association continue the liaisons established by the Task Force with:

   a. The Joint Committee on Standards Development of the American Psychological Association, the American Educational Research Association, and the National Council on Measurement in Education.
   b. The National Institute of Education.
   c. The Educational Testing Service. (The Task Force also recommends that the Association establish similar relationships with other members of the testing industry.)

3. The Association develop a strategy for establishing with other groups and organizations formal alliances for the purpose of combatting deleterious testing practices. These might include the National Association for the Advancement of Colored People, the Association of Black Psychologists, the Mexican-American Legal Defense and Education Fund, the National Urban League, the Civil Rights Commission, parent groups, and other educational organizations, e.g., Association for Supervision and Curriculum Development.

4. The Executive Committee approve the papers entitled "Roles and Responsibilities of Groups Concerned with Student Evaluation Systems," "Why Should All Those Students Take All Those Tests?" and "Guidelines and Cautions for Considering Criterion-Referenced Testing," and that the Association publish them as an information package for distribution to the leadership network and for general availability. It is further recommended that the proposed handbook on "Alternatives to Standardized Testing" and the proposed module on testing for preservice/in-service teacher education be made components of the information package.

5. The Association complete a thorough exploration of the feasibility of a system whereby the NEA certifies tests or other procedures for student or program evaluation. Such exploration is currently under way as a subobjective of the Professional Excellence goal area.

6. The Association temporarily set aside the moratorium on standardized testing as a national objective (as called for in New Business Item 28 adopted in 1972) in order to concentrate its energies in this area on lending support to affiliates as they implement strategies to challenge standardized testing; for example, initiating court actions on behalf of students or teachers, attacking specific test instruments, seeking alliances with other groups which have a vested interest in countering test abuse, cross-committee planning for remediation of problems related to testing, developing negotiation procedures and language dealing with testing issues.

CONTRIBUTORS

CONTRIBUTORS

Dwight Allen, Dean, School of Education, University of Massachusetts, Amherst.

Jean S. Blachford, Classroom Teacher, New Brunswick, New Jersey; Member, NEA Task Force on Testing.

William F. Brazziel, Professor of Higher Education, University of Connecticut, Storrs.

Jose A. Cardenas, Superintendent, Edgewood Independent School District, San Antonio, Texas.

Lupe Castillo, Classroom Teacher, San Francisco, California; Member, NEA Task Force on Testing.

Dorothy Lee Collins, Classroom Teacher (Counselor), San Antonio, Texas; Member, NEA Task Force on Testing.

Charlotte Darehshori, Teacher, Primary Grouping, William Penn Elementary School, Bakersfield, California.

Edward A. De Avila, Director of Educational Planning and Research, Bilingual Children's Television.

Richard F. Docter, Professor of Psychology, California State University, Northridge.

Brenda S. Engel, Visiting Assistant Professor, Lesley College, Cambridge, Massachusetts; Former Public School Art Teacher.

Barbara Havassy, Langley Porter Neuropsychiatric Institute, University of California, San Francisco.

Milton G. Holmen, Professor of Management and Associate Dean, School of Business Administration, University of Southern California, Los Angeles.

Pilialoha Lee Loy, Classroom Teacher, Honolulu, Hawaii; Member, NEA Task Force on Testing.

Bernard McKenna, NEA Instruction and Professional Development.

Jane R. Mercer, Associate Professor of Sociology, University of California, Riverside.

Lawrence Perales, Classroom Teacher, Santa Maria, California; Member, NEA Task Force on Testing.

Frances Quinto, NEA Instruction and Professional Development.

Charles J. Sanders, Classroom Teacher (Secondary Counselor), Millinocket, Maine; Chairperson, NEA Task Force on Testing.

Robert S. Soar, Foundations of Education, Institute for Development of Human Resources, University of Florida.

Ruth M. Soar, Florida Educational Research and Development Council.

Thelma Spencer, Director, Teacher Education Examination Program, Educational Testing Service, Princeton, New Jersey.

Richard J. Stiggins, Assistant Director of Test Development, American College Testing Program; Former Coordinator of Educational Research and Program Evaluation, Edina (Minnesota) Public Schools.

Edwin F. Taylor, Senior Research Scientist, Department of Physics and Division for Study and Research in Education, Massachusetts Institute of Technology.

Robert L. Williams, Director, Black Studies Program, and Professor of Psychology, Washington University, St. Louis, Missouri.

Leroy Wilson, Classroom Teacher, Ocala, Florida; Member, NEA Task Force on Testing.

FOOTNOTES AND REFERENCES

"What's Wrong with Standardized Testing?" by Bernard McKenna

[1] For sources and further explanation of Alfred Binet's work and Lewis Terman and Henry Goddard's work, see Kamin, Leon J. "The Politics of I.Q." *National Elementary Principal* 54: 15-22; March-April 1975.

"Why Should All Those Students Take All Those Tests?"

[1] In *Task Force and Other Reports* presented to the Fifty-Second Representative Assembly of the National Education Association, July 3-6, 1973, Portland, Oregon. pp. 26-46.

[2] House, Ernest R.; Rivers, Wendell; and Stufflebeam, Dan. *An Assessment of the Michigan Accountability System.* Michigan Education Association and National Education Association, March 1974. pp. 14-16.

[3] National Education Association. "Criteria for Evaluating State Education Accountability Systems." Washington, D.C.: the Association, n.d..

[4] Womer, Frank B. *Developing a Large-Scale Assessment Program.* Denver: Cooperative Accountability Project, 1973.

[5] Psychometrics in the strictest sense of the definition has to do with the measurement of mental abilities. It has come to be used much more broadly to define a wide range of activities in assessment and evaluation.

[6] For information on probability samples, see Womer, *op. cit.*

"Guidelines and Cautions for Considering Criterion-Referenced Testing" by Bernard McKenna

[1] Baker, Eva L. "Beyond Objectives: Domain-Referenced Tests for Evaluation and Instructional Improvement." *Educational Technology,* 1973.

[2] Bloom, Benjamin S.; Hastings, J. Thomas; and Madaus, George F. Chapter 11: "The Cooperative Development of Evaluation Systems." *Handbook on Formative and Summative Evaluation of Student Learning.* New York: McGraw-Hill, 1971. pp. 249-58.

[3] Glaser, Robert, and Witko, Anthony J. "Measurement in Learning and Instruction." *Educational Measurement.* (Edited by Robert L. Thorndike.) Washington, D.C.: American Council on Education, 1971. pp. 625-70.

[4] Hively, Wells. "Domain-Referenced Testing." *Educational Technology,* 1973.

[5] House, Ernest R' "Validating a Goal-Priority Instrument." Paper presented at the annual meeting of American Educational Research Association, New Orleans, February 25-March 1, 1973.

[6] _____ ; Rivers, Wendell; and Stufflebeam, Dan. *An Assessment of the Michigan Accountability System.* Michigan Education Association and National Education Association, March 1974.

[7] Klein, Stephen P., and Kosecoff, Jacqueline. *Issues and Procedures in the Development of Criterion-Referenced Tests.* Princeton, N.J.: ERIC Clearinghouse on Tests, Measurement, and Evaluation, September 1973.

[8] Millman, Jason. "How To Make Assessment Plans for Domain-Referenced Tests." *Educational Technology,* 1973.

[9] Popham, W. James, and Husek, R. R. "Implications of Criterion-Referenced Measurement." *Journal of Educational Measurement,* 1969.

[10] Stake, Robert E. "Measuring What Learners Learn." *School Evaluation.* (Edited by Ernest R. House.) Berkeley, Calif.: McCutchan Publishing Corp., 1973.

[11] _____, and Gooler, Dennis. "Measuring Goal Priorities." *School Evaluation.* (Edited by Ernest R. House.) Berkeley, Calif.: McCutchan Publishing Corp., 1973.

[12] Womer, Frank B. "What is Criterion-Referenced Measurement?" IRA Committee on the Evaluation of Reading Tests. 1973.

"Criticisms of Standardrized Testing" by Milton G. Holmen and Richard F. Docter.

[1] Passanella, Ann K.; Manning, Winton H.; and Findikyan, Nurhan. "Criticisms of Testing: I." Unpublished report to Commission on Tests, College Entrance Examination Board, 1967. ED 039 395.

[2] Goslin, David A. "What's Wrong with Tests and Testing." *College Board Review* 65: 12-18; Fall 1967; *College Board Review* 66: 33-37; Winter 1967. ED 039 392.

[3] Holmen, Milton G., and Docter, Richard F. *Educational and Psychological Testing: A Study of the Industry and Its Practices.* New York: Russell Sage Foundation, 1972.

[4] Rosenthal, Robert, and Jacobson, Lenore. *Pygmalion in the Classroom: Teacher Expectation and Pupils' Intellectual Development.* New York: Holt, Rinehart and Winston, 1968.

"Problems in Using Pupil Outcomes for Teacher Evaluation" by Robert S. Soar and Ruth M. Soar;

[1] Anderson, G. J. "Effects of Classroom Social Climate on Individual Learning." *American Educational Research Journal* 7: 135-53; March 1970.

[2] Bereiter, C. "Some Persisting Dilemmas in the Measurement of Change." *Problems in Measuring Change.* (Edited by C. W. Harris.) Madison: University of Wisconsin Press, 1963. p. 3.

[3] Brophy, J. E. *Stability in Teacher Effectiveness.* R & D Report Series 77. Austin: Research and Development Center for Teacher Education, University of Texas, July 1972.

[4] Cronbach, L. J. *Essentials of Psychological Testing.* Second edition. New York: Harper and Brothers, 1960. p. 131.

[5] Flanders, N. A. "The Changing Base of Performance-Based Teaching." *Phi Delta Kappan* 55: 312-15; January 1974.

[6] Garber, M., and Ware, W. B. "The Home Environment as a Predictor of School Achievement." *Theory Into Practice* 11: 190-95; June 1972.

[7] Lord, F. M. "Elementary Models for Measuring Change." *Problems in Measuring Change.* (Edited by C. W. Harris.) Madison: University of Wisconsin Press, 1963. Chapter 2, pp. 21-38.

[8] McDonald, F. J. "The State of the Art in Performance Assessment of Teaching Competence." *Performance Education: Assessment.* (Edited by T. E. Andrews.) Albany: Multi-State Consortium on Performance-Based Teacher Education, New York State Education Department, 1974.

[9] Mayeske, G. W., and others, *A Study of Our Nation's Schools.* U.S. Department of Health, Education, and Welfare, Office of Education, Report No. DHEW-OE-72-142. Washington, D.C.: Government Printing Office, 1972.

[10] Medley, D. M. "Research and Assessment in PBTE." AACTE Leadership Training Conference on Performance-Based Teacher Education. St. Louis, April 30, 1974.

[11] Mosteller, F., and Moynihan, D. P. *On Equality of Educational Opportunity.* New York: Random House, 1972.

[12] Page, E. B. "A Final Footnote on PC and OEO." *Phi Delta Kappan* 54: 575; April 1973.
————. "How We All Failed at Performance Contracting." *Phi Delta Kappan,* 54: 115-17; October 1972.

[13] Rosenshine, Barak. "The Stability of Teacher Effects Upon Student Achievement." *Review of Educational Research* 40: 647-62; December 1970.

[14] Small, Alan A. "Accountability in Victorian England." *Phi Delta Kappan* 53: 438-39; March 1972.

[15] Soar, R. S. "Optimum Teacher-Pupil Interaction for Pupil Growth." *Educational Leadership Research Supplement* 2: 275-80; December, 1968.

[16] Soar, R. S. and Soar, R. M. *Classroom Behavior, Pupil Characteristics, and Pupil Growth for the School Year and for the Summer.* Grant numbers 5 ROI MH 15891 and 5 ROI MH 15626, National Institute of Mental Health, U.S. Department of Health, Education, and Welfare. Gainesville: University of Florida, 1973.

[17] ————. "An Empirical Analysis of Selected Follow Through Programs: An Example of a Process Approach to Evaluation." *Early Childhood Education.* (Edited by I. J. Gordon.) Seventy-first Yearbook, Part II, National Society for the Study of Education. Chicago: University of Chicago Press, 1972. Chapter 11, pp. 229-59.

[18] Solomon, D.; Bezdek, W. E.; and Rosenberg, L. *Teaching Styles and Learning.* Chicago: Center for the Study of Liberal Education of Adults, 1963.

"Use of Tests: Employment and Counseling" by Thelma Spencer.

[1] Black, Hillel. *They Shall Not Pass.* New York: William Morrow & Co., 1963. p. 167.

[2] Wasserman, Miriam. *School Fix, NYC, U.S.A.* New York: Outerbridge and Dienstfrey, 1970. pp. 155-56.

[3] Quoted in Black, *op. cit.,* p. 260.

Report of the NEA Task Force on Testing, 1975.

[1] For supporting arguments, see the first interim report in *Task Force and Other Reports* presented to the Fifty-Second Representative Assembly of the National Education Association, July 3-6, 1973, Portland, Oregon (pp. 26-46).

[2] House, Ernest; Rivers, Wendell; and Stufflebeam, Daniel. *An Assessment of the Michigan Accountability System.* Michigan Education Association and National Education Association, March 1974.

[3] See the section on "Supportive Literature" for a citation of Mercer's study.

[4] "The Awesome Danger of Intelligence Tests." *Ebony* 29: 68-70, 72; August 1974.

[5]Members of the committee are Jean Blachford, Pilialoha Lee Loy, and Lawrence Perales representing the Task Force on Testing; Norman Goldman, director of instruction and professional development, New Jersey Education Association; Margaret Morrison, guidance counselor, Rockville, Maryland; Gene V. Glass of the Laboratory of Educational Research, University of Colorado; and Bernard Bartholomew, Bernard McKenna, and Frances Quinto, NEA staff.